Palgrave Studies in Comics and Graphic Novels

Series Editor
Roger Sabin
University of the Arts London
London
United Kingdom

This series concerns Comics Studies—with a capital "c" and a capital "s." It feels good to write it that way. From emerging as a fringe interest within Literature and Media/Cultural Studies departments, to becoming a minor field, to maturing into the fastest growing field in the Humanities, to becoming a nascent *discipline*, the journey has been a hard but spectacular one. Those capital letters have been earned.

Palgrave Studies in Comics and Graphic Novels covers all aspects of the comic strip, comic book, and graphic novel, explored through clear and informative texts offering expansive coverage and theoretical sophistication. It is international in scope and provides a space in which scholars from all backgrounds can present new thinking about politics, history, aesthetics, production, distribution, and reception as well as the digital realm. Books appear in one of two forms: traditional monographs of 60,000 to 90,000 words and shorter works (Palgrave Pivots) of 20,000 to 50,000 words. All are rigorously peer-reviewed. Palgrave Pivots include new takes on theory, concise histories, and—not least—considered provocations. After all, Comics Studies may have come a long way, but it can't progress without a little prodding.

Series Editor Roger Sabin is Professor of Popular Culture at the University of the Arts London, UK. His books include *Adult Comics: An Introduction and Comics, Comix and Graphic Novels*, and his recent research into nineteenth-century comics is award-winning. He serves on the boards of the main academic journals in the field and reviews graphic novels for the international media.

More information about this series at
http://www.springer.com/series/14643

Ian Gordon

Kid Comic Strips

A Genre Across Four Countries

palgrave
macmillan

Ian Gordon
Department of History
National University of Singapore
Singapore, Singapore

Palgrave Studies in Comics and Graphic Novels
ISBN 978-1-137-56197-8   ISBN 978-1-137-55580-9 (eBook)
DOI 10.1057/978-1-137-55580-9

Library of Congress Control Number: 2016956661

Cover illustration: Pattern adapted from an Indian cotton print produced in the 19th century

Printed on acid-free paper

This Palgrave Pivot imprint is published by Springer Nature
The registered company is Nature America Inc.
The registered company address is: 1 New York Plaza, New York, NY 10004, U.S.A.

For Joanne

Acknowledgments

My thanks to the staff of the State Library of NSW for making the original bound volumes available. In 1987, John Graham graciously allowed access. In 2015, Royce Propert and Steve Richards arranged access. My thanks also to Anne Doherty, Maggie Patton, and Alison Wishart.

My thanks to the staff of the British Library, somewhat bemused at a researcher looking at the *Beano*, but always professional and courteous.

My thanks also to the staff of the *New York Public Library*, who were likewise always professional and courteous.

My thanks to Beatriz Sequeira de Carvalho for assistance with details about Buster Brown in Brazil.

This work was supported by the Ministry of Education, Republic of Singapore, AcRF Tier 1 grant R-110-000-077-112

CONTENTS

LIST OF FIGURES

CHAPTER 1

Why Kid Comics

Abstract The chapter argues that by comparing comics from different countries it is possible to understand just what features American comic strips have contributed to the international form of comic art. The chapter offers a brief account of the passage of American comics to France, Italy and Brazil and a slight history of comics in Britain and Australia.

Keywords Buster Brown · Word Balloons · Translation

Comics are international phenomena. To be sure they go by different names like *bande dessinée, manga, fumetto, las historietas,* and *quadrinhos,* and they come in different forms such as comic strips (with and without word balloons), comic books, and other forms of graphic sequential narrative, but the form itself is fairly ubiquitous. In the last 20 years or so, a broad group of scholars from across the world has produced an array of work detailing histories and analyzing the form and its impact to the extent that comics scholarship has become a field of inquiry. In this flurry of activity, many national histories have been told and the formal aspects of comics, panels, pages, word balloons, and the like, analyzed and dissected.

© The Author(s) 2016
I. Gordon, *Kid Comic Strips*, Palgrave Studies in Comics
and Graphic Novels, DOI 10.1057/978-1-137-55580-9_1

KID COMICS

A comparative study of kid comic strips across four different countries is an attempt to consider genre in comics as a way to approach international histories of comics. Kid comics refers to comics featuring kids, which may or may not have been read by children, but the majority of the works I study were aimed at audiences of diverse ages. In this book, I offer three comparative studies: The American strip *Skippy* with the Australian strip *Ginger Meggs*, the Perry Winkle Sunday episodes of the American strip *Winnie Winkle* with the French translation of that strip as *Bicot*, and both the American and British *Dennis the Menace* comics. These are but six kid comics that can usefully be compared and my study is exploratory rather than exhaustive.

The impact of recent scholarship on comics has led to more nuanced understandings of the way they developed in many countries. Gone are the days when a work could assert "the American newspaper comic strip . . . is a major innovation and creative cultural accomplishment of the United States, one that has spread around the world" seemingly disinterested in the long European antecedents that helped give birth to, and shape, American comics. And this despite acknowledging that Rudolph Dirk's early American comic strip *The Katzenjammer Kids* "had originally been copied directly from the two schrecklichkinder of [Wilhelm] Busch."[1] The authors of this assessment Bill Blackbeard and Martin Williams did not make it clear if their meaning was that American comics spread around the world, or if they meant that comics spread from America to the world. Indeed, in 1977, it may have seemed to them that the two amounted to the same thing. In any case, in American accounts of comics the latter view was commonly referenced. Their statement and others like it were a little too quick to attribute accomplishments to the USA that were broader in origin. Scholars such as David Kunzle and Thierry Smoldren have done much to show the European roots of American comics and while popular perceptions still abound, that somehow comic strips are uniquely American, and Richard Outcault's character the Yellow Kid the first comic strip, academics have moved on from this limited view.[2] Studying kid comic strips across four countries helps shed more light on just what American comics contributed to the development of the form.

What marked American comic strips and made them different from comics elsewhere was their place in mass circulated newspapers. This gave American comic art a distinctively commercial bent and those comics were a constitutive element in shaping a culture of consumption in America. The importance of the Yellow Kid had nothing to do with the formal properties of comics, or the creation of strips in sequential panels as the form of newspaper comic strips, or the use of word balloons, since none of these were quintessential features of that comic. What was important was the distinctive character. When the American newspaper comic strip eventually coalesced into a recognizable form in the first six months of 1901, they had three key features: a distinctive character, sequential panels, and mostly used word balloons. All these features of course had existed in earlier European comic art. What made the American comics different was that they were ongoing features that appeared on a regular schedule and were so essential to the creation of mass circulated newspapers, the mass media, that it is difficult to separate the two.[3]

Kid comics were important to the development of comic strips in American newspapers and this had an international character. Busch's *Max und Moritz* inspired Dirks's concept for the *Katzenjammer Kids* and quite early in their existence American comic strips were exported to other countries. This importing of American comics did not mean those countries had no comics traditions before the arrival of comics American style. Richard Outcault's *Buster Brown* comic strip, which he began in 1902, and that was one of the most widely distributed comic strips in America, was sold by the Hearst syndicate to other countries such as Italy, France, and Brazil. In Italy, *Buster Brown* ran in *Corriere dei Piccoli* under the title *Mimmo Mammolo*. Often the word balloons that Outcault used were removed and rhyming captions used under the panels. Alex Valente discussed this comic along with several others at a conference in Glasgow in 2013. He focused on issues of translation and highlighted the problems of translating idioms. He also pointed to the way that onomatopoeia presented special problems in translation, in that the sounds these represent might not be the way such sounds are heard or understood in other languages.[4] In France, *Buster Brown* appeared in comics albums published by Hachette. These volumes appear to be translations of American edition of Buster's weekly strips that were published by F. A. Stokes and later Cupples & Leon. According to Antoine Sausverd, on his *Topfferiana* web site, in 1905 the weekly children's supplement of the Parisian newspaper *Le Petit Journal, Le Petit Journal illustré de la jeunesse* ran an imitation Buster Brown titled "Les exploits de Turc, Jacasse et Cie" an example of which from December 24, 1905, he reproduces. This comic mostly used captions and not word balloons, but the last panel had the faux Buster talking with his dog and used word balloons.[5]

In Brazil, Renato de Castro adapted Buster Brown, apparently by tracing Outcault's strips, for the children's publication *O Tico-Tico* that commenced publication on October 1, 1905. In the *O Tico-Tico* version, Buster Brown became Chiquinho and his dog Tige, Jagunço. The episode appearing in the first issue of *O Tico-Tico*, "The Misadventures of Chiquinho: The Race With Jagunço" was a rather crude rendering, but nonetheless recognizable as Buster Brown. Chiquinho did not remain a simple copy of Buster Brown with *O Tico-Tico*'s artists reworking it in several fashions. For instance, in 1909, several issues of the strip featured a mash-up of Buster Brown and Winsor McCay's *Little Nemo in Slumberland*. With the advent of World War I and difficulties in obtaining the America originals, Luis Gomes Loureiro, who had early taken over Chiquinho from de Castro, began to create material from scratch, thereby creating something different and more Brazilian in character. Outside of Brazil, Chiquinho and its impact remains little studied.[6]

The history of Buster Brown then is mostly told in national frameworks with some reference in Italian, France, and Brazilian reflections on the character of his American origins. Those writing on the American history of Buster Brown, myself included, have largely ignored or been unaware of the extent of the characters' transnational dimensions. The sort of language skills and research time needed to address the international dimensions of Buster Brown are daunting and it is probably beyond the reach of a single scholar to do so. Nonetheless, Buster Brown was not the only American comic strip to have an international dimension and there are other ways at coming at the issue of the impact of kid comics in different countries.

At first it might seem surprising that American comics were not exported to English-speaking countries such as Britain or Australia. Certainly papers in Canada carried American comic strips. For instance, *The Ottawa Journal* carried Hearst strips like *Mutt and Jeff* and *Bringing Up Father* by 1915. The contiguous nature of the two North American countries probably accounts for this spread north. Both Britain and Australia had distinctive comics traditions of their own and this might explain the relative lack of imports. Roger Sabin has shown the importance of Ally Sloper, and the eponymous comic weekly, *Ally Sloper's Half Holiday*, to the development of the form in Britain.[7] Weekly comic magazines were more important in Britain to the development of comic art and it was not until 1915 that the first daily comic strip, *Teddy Tail*, appeared in the *Daily Mail*.[8] Australia developed a tradition of its own in which all forms of comics and their artists came together for many years in the Black and White Artists' Club.[9] But these traditions had a heavy dose of American influence because so much of the work for these artists flowed from *The Bulletin* magazine, which at its founding in 1880 had imported American printers trained in photo engraving, and Livingston Hopkins an artist best known then for his work for the New York-based illustrated humor journal, *Judge*.[10] Despite these American influences, comic strips did not develop in Australia until the 1920s. But there were some comics weekly magazines, in the manner of such British publications, including *Vumps* and *The Comic Australian*. Aimed at children, this latter publication ran for two years from 1911 to 1913. In its first issue, the magazine published a one-off comic strip, *Jim and Jam, Bushrangers Bold*, which transposed *Max und Moritz* or the *Katzenjammer Kids*, to the Australian bush as outlaws. The artist of this strip Hugh McCrae, a poet, actor and essayist, later lived in New York where he shared an apartment with fellow Australian Pat Sullivan, the creator of *Felix the Cat*. Late in life, McCrae told the story that Sullivan had asked him to draw that cartoon and comic, which he passed up, much to his regret.[11] Whether or not the story is true, Sullivan's success and McCrae's presence in New York is indicative of the transnational nature of comic art and artists early in the twentieth century. In Australia on November 13, 1921, the *Sunday Sun* in Sydney commenced publishing a comic strip supplement that included *Us Fellers*, a comic strip better known by its lead character, and later title, *Ginger Meggs*. All the comic strips in the *Sunday Sun* were Australian in origin, but the notion of a Sunday comics supplement was an American import.

The eminent historian Eugene Weber recounts that in France the Parisian newspapers only started to circulate nationally during World War I.[12] By the 1920s these newspapers, such as *Le Petit Journal*, carried comic strips in their illustrated supplement. These comic strips, like *Fouinard et sa bande* and *Les aventures de fricot*, lacked word balloons and used narrative text underneath the panels. *Quart de Brie et Sac a Puces,* another of the strips carried by *Le Petit Journal*, beginning January 3, 1926, and signed by Zep, featured a dog, Sac a Puces (Flea Bag) who winked from the masthead in a manner similar to Buster Brown's dog Tige (Fig. 1.1).[13] But this strip too did not use word balloons. The first comic strips to use word balloons on a regular basis in French newspapers were *Bicot* and *La famille Mirliton* in *Excelsior Dimanche* (later *Le Dimanche Illustré*). Like *Bicot, La famille Mirliton*, more familiar as *The Gumps*, was an American strip from the *Chicago Tribune*. In 1925,

Zig et Puce by Frenchman Alain Saint-Ogan joined those two strips and was most likely the first French comic strip to use word balloons on a regular basis. Both Thierry Smolderen and Pascal Lefèvre have written on the development of word balloons. Smolderen traces the history of word balloon like instruments and makes a case for their appearance in America in the early 1900s as solving a need to give voice to characters. Partially this need arose in response to Thomas Edison's development of the phonograph and the resulting fascination with the reproduction of sound. Lefèvre sees word balloons as part of a process "from a culture that privileged the written word to a more visual oriented mass culture in the second part of the 20th century." This change came later in Europe partially at least because comics were regarded as children's fare and as having an educational function so that captions beneath panels were seen as more educational.[14] *Bicot* played an important role in this growing use of word balloons in France. Hachette collected the strip into 14 albums published annually between 1926 and 1939, and then later reprinted by other publishers in the 1960s and 1970s. *La famille Mirliton* on the other hand has very little presence beyond its initial appearance in *Le Dimanche Illustré.*

As important as *Bicot* may have been in the acceptance of word balloons in French comic art, my purpose in examining *Bicot* is more for the way that humor played out in different fashions in France and America and not so much on the different comics traditions of those countries, although clearly it is hard to separate the two. Likewise in Britain, separating the sort of comics that developed and the humor they displayed from the technical form they took is no simple matter. The British *Dennis the Menace* for instance appeared in the *Beano,* a comics weekly for children that D. C. Thomson commenced publishing on July 30, 1938. The *Beano* was a stable mate to *The Dandy* that had begun

Fig. 1.1 *Quart de Brie et Sac a Puces, Le Petit Journal,* January 3, 1926

publishing on December 4, 1937. The use of word balloons, rather than text beneath the panels, distinguished *The Dandy* from other British comics weeklies at that time. The *Beano* followed suit, although both comics also contained strips that did not use word balloons. Comparing the British *Dennis* with the American *Dennis* requires some consideration of formal properties beyond their different forms of publication because the American comic in its daily incarnation is a single panel and does not use word balloons.

HUMOR

There are certain jokes that work across cultures with little need for translation. In an article discussing the relationship between early French film and *bande dessinée* Lance Rickman displays that the sight gag of a gardener using a hose to spray water, having it blocked by a prankster, looking at the nozzle to see why it had stopped and then being sprayed with water when the prankster unblocked the hose, worked in several cultures and appeared in different forms of comics including the *Katzenjammer Kids* and *Happy Hooligan* comic strips in America.[15] Many gags are rather common. For instance, balls through window gags are extremely common and the Michigan State University Library has catalogue entries for at least 35 spread over a number of years.[16] The comics I look at in this book worked numerous common jokes, sometimes providing great mirth and at other times incredible banality. Some of the gags are innocuous and others display racism and a casual misogyny. My point in this book is not to examine, say the still funny gags for what makes them funny, but to show how kid comics in different cultures worked a vein of humor. What was similar and what was different and how does that help us understand comics as an international art form. I did not expect Martin Branner's racist humor in his Perry Winkle comics to translate into French and thought the strips in question would not have appeared in France. I was somewhat surprised that they did, not because I think the French as a people any less racist than the rest of the world, but because I thought the humor would be too distinctly American to translate. That some of it translated so easily was a revelation and that some of these translations require a more complex understanding of how culture takes shape went to the heart of this book's themes.

SOURCES AND METHODOLOGY

I chose the six comics I examine in this book partially for ease of access and partially for familiarity. For the first chapter I turned to *Skippy* and *Ginger Meggs* because the recent three volumes of Skippy dailies from IDW provided at hand research material. The years 1925–1933 that these volumes cover determined the 1920s and early 1930s as a focal point for two of my chapters. My own work on Ginger Meggs from an earlier project meant that I had a strong familiarity with that strip and more importantly I had heard from several Australian comic strip artists that *Skippy* had influenced several Australian comics artists. Collecting a comparable sample of *Ginger Meggs* strips to analyze required a trip to the State Library of NSW in Sydney, Australia, where fortunately I was able to use my phone to photograph over 400 strips in the original bound newspaper volumes. With Perry Winkle and *Bicot* I had the good fortune to discover the digital collection of *Excelsior Dimanche – Le Dimanche Illustré* at Cité internationale de la bande dessinée et de l'image, which although not complete does cover over 85 % of issues.[17] I read most of *Winnie Winkle* 25 years ago for my doctoral research, but concentrated on the daily strips since mostly the Sunday strips featuring Perry had something of a separate continuity. These comics are available in the *Chicago Tribune* through the ProQuest database, which has certain advantages over looking at them on microfilm that was the only way they were available to me in 1991. The main advantage of course is that I could do the work from where I live rather than traveling to the USA. I did indeed spend time in America to track down some Sunday episodes of *Skippy* and the American *Dennis the Menace* comics. Fortunately. Fanatgraphics has produced six volumes of the daily *Dennis the Menace* covering the years from his origin in 1951 to 1963. These volumes set the timeframe for my study of the *Menaces*. For the British *Dennis the Menace* I visited the British Library where I was again able to use my phone to photograph the strip in their collection of the *Beano*. Having spent many months in the early 1990s hunched over a microfilm reader in the Library of Congress locating comic strips in newspaper reels, getting nauseous in the process from the slow scrolling, this research process was on the whole more enjoyable. But the point here is that the process has been different from my own earlier work on comic strips. Working with a large amount of visual material has its own unique challenges for organization of research materials and working through issues by comparing and contrasting sources. Collections of comic strips make it vastly easier for a researcher to get through a volume of material in far quicker time. Moreover, it is easier to keep track of themes and the like because the material is at hand. Likewise, photographing and downloading reference copies, which can be stored on a computer for later reference, is much easier than photostatting from microfilm reels. All-round, as a researcher I gathered, and could consult, a large reference base of material that simply would not have been possible in earlier years. With this sort of research, ideas germinate more readily and can be cross-referenced against sources immediately. The increasing availability of digital archives also greatly aids such a project. This does not mean scholarship is easier, but it does mean that projects can now be done that were beyond the capacity of individuals working with small budgets in years gone by. Nonetheless, it is still far easier to work with printed volumes and the publishers of comic strip reprints deserve researchers' support and gratitude.

In this book I have focused on the comics on the page. All of these strips had some incarnations off the page, as licensed goods, Department store window displays, television series (live action and animated), and films. Each of these other media adds complexity to the characters and play out in a manner probably better understood through a study of individual characters than in a broad comparative study like this book. For instance, in the case of Ginger Meggs, his status as an icon of Australian identity means that he crops up in unlikely places, such as editorial cartoons, that complicate any reading of the character because so many values can be attributed to him through his other iterations.[18]

This study then is suggestive of ways to approach the international history of comics. By focusing on a genre, Kid Comics, I show that issues of transmission of one culture to another are not simply matters of linear development or declensions. Instead, multiple factors are at work and a comparative approach sheds light of shared traditions and cultural differences to produce a more nuanced understanding of both the similarities and difference between comics from different countries.

NOTES

1. Bill Blackbeard and Martin Williams, *The Smithsonian Collection of Newspaper Comics* (Washington, DC: Smithsonian Institution Press, 1977), flyleaf, 19. The Hanoverian artist Wilhelm Busch published his illustrated story *Max und Moritz* in 1865.
2. David Kunzle, *History of the Comic Strip: Vol. 1, The Early Comic Strip* (Berkeley: University of California Press, 1973) and *History of the Comic Strip:*

Vol. 2, The Nineteenth Century (Berkeley: University of California Press, 1990): Thierry Smolderen, *Naissances de la bande dessinée: de William Hogarth à Winsor McCay* (Brussels: Les Impressions Nouvelles, 2009) and *The Origins of Comics: From William Hogarth to Winsor McCay* (Jackson: University Press of Mississippi, 2014).

3. Here I am restating in bold terms an argument I made more subtly, perhaps too subtly, in *Comic Strips and Consumer Culture, 1890–1945* (Washington, DC: Smithsonian Institution Press, 1998).

4. Alex Valente, "Translating Humour in Comics, from Italian to English to Italian," presented at International Comics and Graphic Novel and International Bande Dessinée Society, Joint Conference, Glasgow and Dundee, June 24–28, 2013.

5. Antoine Sausverd, "La beauté convulsive de Buster Brown," *Topfferiana*, October 30, 2014, http://www.topfferiana.fr/2014/10/la-beaute-convulsive-de-buster-brown/

6. Waldomiro Vergueiro, "Children's comics in Brazil: From *Chiquinho* to *Mônica*, a Difficult Journey," *International Journal of Comic Art*, Vol. 1 no. 1 (1999): 171–186; Álvaro Moya *História da História em Quadrinhos*. 3ª Edição. São Paulo: Brasiliense, 1994, 25. See also Matthew Maculotti, "Chiquinho 'in Slumberland': quando Buster Brown fu Little Nemo," *bambini&topi*, August 19, 2014, http://www.bambinietopi.it/2014/08/chiquinho-in-slumberland-quando-buster.html.

7. Roger Sabin, "Ally Sloper: The First Comics Superstar?," *Image & Narrative*, Vol. 4, No. 1 (October 2003), http://www.imageandnarrative.be/inarchive/graphicnovel/rogersabin.htm; David Kunzle, "Marie Duval: A Caricaturist Rediscovered," *Woman's Art Journal*, Vol. 7, No. 1 (Spring–Summer, 1986): 26–31; Peter Bailey, "Ally Sloper's Half-Holiday: Comic Art in the 1880s," *History Workshop*, Vol. 16, No. 1 (1983): 4–31.

8. George Perry and Alan Aldridge, *The Penguin Book of Comics: A Slight History* (Harmondsworth: Penguin Books, 1971), 201.

9. Vane Lindesay, *Drawing from Life: A History of the Australian Black and White Artists' Club* (Sydney: State Library of New South Wales Press, 1994).

10. Ian Gordon, "From the Bulletin to Comics: Comic Art in Australia, 1890–1950," in *Bonzer: Australian Comics, 1900s–1990s*. Annette Shiell, editor (Redhill South, VIC: Elgua Media, 1999), 1–14.

11. C. R. Bradish, "The Poetic," *Sydney Morning Herald*, May 3, 1953, 9.

12. Eugene Weber, *Peasants Into Frenchmen: The Modernization of Rural France, 1870–1914* (Palo Alto: Stanford University Press, 1976), 565–566, note 46.

13. *Le Petit Journal Illustré*, December 25, 1920, http://gallica.bnf.fr/ark:/12148/bpt6k717451x/f12.item.r=Le%20Petit%20journal%20illustr%C3%A9: *Le Petit Journal Illustré*, December 20, 1925, http://gallica.bnf.fr/ark:/12148/bpt6k717711g/f9.item; *Le Petit Journal Illustré*, December

27, 1925, http://gallica.bnf.fr/ark:/12148/bpt6k717712v/f8.item; *Le Petit Journal Illustré*, January 3, 1926, http://gallica.bnf.fr/ark:/12148/bpt6k7177137/f9.item.

14. Thierry Smolderen, "Of Labels, Loops, and Bubbles: Solving the Historical Puzzle of the Speech Balloon," *Comic Art*, No. 8 (Summer 2006): 90–113; Pascal Lefèvre, "The Battle Over the Balloon: The Conflictual Institutionalization of the Speech Balloon in Various European Cultures," *Image & Narrative*, Vol. 7, No. 1 (July 2006), http://www.imageandnarra tive.be/inarchive/painting/pascal_levevre.htm.
15. Lance Rickman, "Bande dessiné and the Cinematograph: Visual Narrative in 1895," *European Comic Art*, Vol. 1 (Spring 2008): 1–19.
16. Michigan State university Library, Comic Art Collection, http://comics.lib.msu.edu/rri/brri/ballo.htm#btw.
17. Les collections numérisées, Cité internationale de la bande dessinée et de l'image, http://collections.citebd.org/in/faces/details.xhtml?id=46d2e8f5-889f-4b1e-a3b0-2f213a3e4e6f.
18. Ian Gordon, "The Symbol of a Nation: Ginger Meggs and Australian National Identity," *Journal of Australian Studies*, Vol. 16, No. 34 (September 1992): 1–14.

CHAPTER 2

America and Australia: Skippy and Ginger Meggs

Abstract This chapter compares and contrasts the way artists James Bancks and Percy Crosbie used similar humor tropes, such as broken window gags, in their respective comic strips *Ginger Meggs* and *Skippy*. It also examines the different styles needed in a daily and a Sunday comic strip. The two strips shared much and yet each had a distinctive type of humor that requires some familiarity with the culture of origin to fully comprehend.

Keywords James Bancks · Percy Crosby · Ginger Meggs · Skippy · Australia

In trying to develop an international history of comics through a study of a particular genre, like kid comic strips, it is useful to compare strips from countries that had certain cultural similarities and yet other distinct differences. Australia, a country with a population of six and a half million in 1930, shared some cultural similarities with the USA. English was the dominant language in both the countries. But the USA with a population of 123 million was more diverse both racially and geographically. Australia was an urban society, and despite myths of a rugged bush tradition, had always been so, but the country had only six major urban centers and none of these had over a million people. The countries then were of a different scale and American cities were culturally different from Australian cities

© The Author(s) 2016   13
I. Gordon, *Kid Comic Strips*, Palgrave Studies in Comics
and Graphic Novels, DOI 10.1057/978-1-137-55580-9_2

because of their more diverse makeup. Although Australia had a strong cartoon art tradition dating from the 1890s, newspaper owners did not start using comic strips to promote their Sunday editions until the 1920s. Of these, the most successful was a strip that centered on the character Ginger Meggs, who though by no means a copy, engaged in similar sorts of larks as the American character Skippy.

James Bancks, the creator of *Ginger Meggs*, and Percy Crosby, the creator of *Skippy*, were born in 1889 and 1891, respectively. Both left school in their mid-teens and only began formal art lessons after finding work as cartoonists. Both Bancks and Crosby spent a good portion of their childhoods growing up in the suburban reaches of cities. Bancks grew up in Hornsby at the end of the North Shore Railway line in Sydney, Australia. The line constructed in the 1890s transformed the area, but Hornsby at the time still had a considerable rural quality. Crosby's family moved from Brooklyn to Richmond Hill in Queens a few years after his birth. Richmond Hill too retained something of a rural character, but New York City was developing at a pace that rapidly outstripped that of Sydney, even if the growth in Sydney was of a greater increase percentage wise, the scale of New York's growth was of a greater weight. For instance, New York in 1870 had a population of around 1.2 million and Sydney 127,000. By 1900, New York's population was almost 3.5 million and Sydney's 481,000.[1] Bancks and Crosby found success in the 1920s with comic strips after doing a variety of other work.

Bancks's comic strip *Us Fellers* commenced on November 13, 1921, in the Sydney *Sunday Sun*. Originally focused on Gladsome Gladys, the conceit of the strip was that Glady's charms won the heart of adults after misadventures by the group of kids she played with. Indeed, in the first episode of the strip Gladys charms the older gentleman whose window has been broken by a tremendous hit (a six) by Lanky off the googly bowler, an as-yet-unnamed Ginger Meggs during a backyard cricket match. On Christmas Day 1921, Bancks gave the bowler a name "Ginger Smith." By April 23, 1922, the name, and the focus of the strip, shifted to Ginger Meggs. Eventually, in November 1939, Bancks formally retitled the strip *Ginger Meggs*. Ginger Meggs outlived its artist and has run uninterrupted since 1921 with four artists after Bancks continuing the strip. At various times Ginger has been held up as the epitome of Australia.[2]

Crosby's *Skippy* commenced as a weekly featured in *Life* magazine in March 1923. The strip was a culmination of his earlier work on numerous features like *Back of the Flats* and strips such as *Beany and the Gang* and

The Clancy Kids. Johnson Features began syndicating a daily version of *Skippy* in June 1925 and the strip ran until 1945. In October 1926 King Features began syndicating a Sunday version and from April 1929 King took charge of the daily syndication as well.[3] Comics artists like Jules Feiffer, Jerry Robinson, Charles Schulz, and Walt Kelly have celebrated *Skippy* as a high point of the art form. *Pogo, Peanuts,* and even *Calvin and Hobbes* clearly drew inspiration from Skippy's motifs and flights of fancy. This study is drawn from an examination of the three volumes of *Skippy* daily comic strips reprinted by IDW that cover 1925–1933, *Skippy* Sunday strips from 1929 to 1933, and two readings at the State Library of New South Wales of the published *Ginger Meggs* strips, once in 1987 when I read all the strips from 1921 to 1987 and a more recent visit during which I photographed all available strips from 1921 to 1933.

BREAKING WINDOWS

Both *Ginger Meggs* and *Skippy* located their protagonists in suburban areas that certainly evoked the Hornsby and Richmond Hill childhoods of their creators. The two strips worked several similar themes, of which two stand out in particular: the broken window joke and the use of soap box carts, or billy carts as Australians call them, as the loci of humor. The broken window joke in the first episode of *Ginger Meggs* in 1921 was a staple of kid comic strips and both Bancks and Crosby worked this theme on numerous occasions in their strips. The broken window theme is so common that most kid strips deployed it at some time. For instance, on September 28, 1924, Martin Branner used a broken window gag in the American strip *Winnie Winkle* and despite the American football (gridiron) theme that strip appeared in French as *Bicot* on November 2, 1924. The basic gag of that strip was that once the ball had gone through the window of a neighbor Perry Winkle (Bicot in France) and his friends claimed ignorance of the ball. The outraged neighbor, when challenged about the likelihood of a ball traveling so far as to break his window, demonstrated that possibility with an almighty kick. The payoff was that the neighbor broke another of his windows and his wife led him away for a scolding.

In Ginger's case, Bancks returned to the broken window gag on April 30, 1922. In this full-page strip over 12 panels Bancks had Ginger playing with a new football in the street. He displays his kicking prowess to his love interest Min and in the first instance hits a pedestrian. After his dog Mike retrieves the ball Ginger again sets out to display his skill but manages to kick the ball through the window of the fruiterer Joe Spagoni. Discovering Ginger's name on the ball Joe goes to the Meggs house to complain to Ginger's mother. The joke is simply that Ginger is in trouble. But some of the jokes play out racially, with Joe being a stereotypical Italian Australian seller of fruits and vegetables. In Australia, such stereotypes continued well into the twenty-first century, along with what seems a mostly British and Australian retailing experience: the greengrocer. Crosby told similar jokes. The cover of the IDW collection of *Skippy* dailies from 1925 to 1927 is an image of Skippy on the run with an arm full of fruit being chased by what could be an American Italian fruitier. On September 25, 1926, Crosby had Skippy ruminate in a two-panel episode: "To me stealin' is very disgustful" and then in front of a fruit stand "Besides ya can never tell when Tony's watchin'." The Italian fruit seller on the street corner had become a staple of New York life by 1895, with estimates of up to 10,000 Italian Americans pursuing the calling, so this reference to Tony seems likely to be to an Italian fruit seller.[4]

Despite these shared themes, a key difference between the two strips was that for a daily strip Crosby needed a more economical style in setting up and delivering his gag. Crosby varied the number of panels he used sometimes delivering the whole scene in a single panel and other times taking up to four panels. Before 1923, Bancks's Ginger Meggs appeared in a variety of panel lengths and in half-page and full-page versions. But by 1923, Bancks settled in to a full-page and 12-panel form.

The difference between a daily strip and a Sunday strip can be seen in Bancks's April 30, 1922, broken window strip and Crosby's November 21, 1925, similarly themed *Skippy* strip. Bancks could effectively tell two stories in his 12 panels: the escape from the man who wished to call the police with the conclusion of Mike rescuing the ball, and the breaking of Joe's window and Ginger's coming punishment from his mother, Mum in Australian English. Crosby in two panels went straight to the heart of the humor. In the first panel Skippy whacks a golf ball that breaks a shop window. In the second the shopkeeper responds in horror and Skippy hightails it saying: "Darn it! Another ball lost." Crosby's strip is a short sharp joke and Bancks's a small narrative. Both episodes though connect to the large *mise-en-scène* of the particular comic strip. In Ginger's case the episode shapes a coming encounter between Ginger and his Mum. The first episode of *Us Fellers* that moved attention away from Gladys to Ginger, "Wimmin Have No Sense of Humour," dealt with the relationship between Ginger and his mother. And although Sarah Meggs would soften over the years, as indeed did the general level of mayhem and violence in the strip, that relationship existed at the core of the strip in its heyday and into the late twentieth century. This particular strip established one of *Ginger Meggs's* common tropes: transgression by Ginger and judgment and retribution by Mum. In Skippy's case, the quip about losing another ball ties to the moment when he is running away clearly understanding he has done wrong. The humor relies on the instant recognition that the broken window is certainly a bigger problem than the lost ball. For Crosby, the humor of the moment derived from the lightness of the quip when mixed with the apparent seriousness of the situation. The *Skippy* strip of December 29, 1925, offers another broken window gag example. In five panels Crosby had Skippy playing with a pogo stick. In the fourth panel Skippy smashes through the window of a Drug Store. In the fifth panel a word balloon emerges from the broken window with Skippy saying "I . . . I'll have a T . . . Two cents stamp."

As much as Crosby liked incongruity between visual action and the words spoken as a trope to carry his humor he did use the broken window theme as a means to tell other types of gags. In a single panel of October 21, 1926, Crosby has Skippy attempting what looks like a lateral pass in a street game of football. The ball smashes through a butcher's shop window and one of Skippy's playmates says to the startled butcher "what's the matter with ya Mr. Zookman aint playin'?" We know Skippy has thrown the ball because the lines that depict motion emanate from Skippy's arms and trace the flight of the ball to the window where Crosby depicts the breakage through small shards of glass that we read as flying outward. The panel flows elegantly from left to right with the smashed window just slightly off center to the right and the three-dimensional framing of the window producing the effect of a panel for the butcher and a mini panel for Skippy's teammate. Crosby placed two other boys at the top of the panel, one of whom is already running for it, and the other comments on the action, "What a pass that might o' been." Skippy himself comments on the situation that, "I never seen a store yet, but what it wasn't in the way." In a single panel then, Crosby tells the story of a street game of football gone wrong, how the action unfolded, the response of the aggrieved party, and the general difficulties of street games. On February 24, 1927, Crosby offered a street baseball version of this joke, again in a single panel and laid out somewhat in the same fashion. To the left of the panel, and in the background, a catcher stands. In front of him a set of lines depict a hit and a set of motion lines indicate the ball as flown to and through a shop window, possibly the same unfortunate Mr. Zookman given the similar alignment of the streetscape. In the left foreground a figure has advanced, noted through another set of motion lines and a dropped bat. To the right of the panel in the foreground, Skippy wearing a fielding mitt holds up two fingers and announces "hereafter only two bases on that" neatly establishing a ground rule double for the play in street baseball. These two episodes are more narratives of the suburban lives of children and the contested spaces of streets in such locales as the desire to play trumps the suitability of the location. Pointedly in these early strips, cars did not feature as a threat to child safety and rather it is the children who are a threat to suburban commerce.

The shift on locale of breaking windows from backyard activities in Perry/Bicot and Ginger's early cases to commercial suburban streets tells us something about the development of satellite areas to large cities and the increased need to display goods in shops to lure consumers inside. In a sense then, such jokes represented the shift from producerist societies, where goods were purchased to meet needs, to consumerist societies where a demand had to be created for goods beyond that of need. In a March 26, 1932 episode of *Skippy*, Crosby showed the open fields previously used for playing being filled with billboards to advertise products. A November 2, 1924 episode of *Ginger Meggs* captures some of this need to advertise and display good, and the as yet not taken for granted use of shop front display windows. Ginger's friend Bennie tells him that Tiger Kelly, the older local bully and Ginger's arch nemesis, is washing a store's window. Ginger rushes to make fun of Tiger, but takes a beating at his hands. Later when Tiger is washing the inside of the windows Ginger revisits and has his revenge when Tiger momentarily spatially confused tries to kick Ginger forgetting the presence of the window, which of course breaks. Sitting on the roof of his house later, Ginger and Bennie have a good view of Tiger being led away by the police. While some artistic license is present in this strip, it is not too much of a stretch of the imagination to envisage such a scenario occurring in suburban Hornsby, or indeed Richmond Hill, even in the 1920s. With a 12-panel Sunday comic strip Banck's had the space, which in his dailies Crosby lacked, to tell such a story.

Crosby though with a daily strip to create used the ball through the window scenario many times more than Bancks. A December 22, 1928 strip has a nice display of wit from Skippy. Caught by a shopkeeper after breaking a window and accused of thinking he could run away without being caught, Skippy replies "Oh, no, sir! I was just runnin' home for the money so's I could pay for it." Between March 1931 and October 1933, Crosby hit a particularly rich vein of ideas and eight strips used the set up. These strips fit two broad categories: playing in the street and playing at home. These two categories could alternatively be labeled playing with others and playing alone since the streets were the location for Skippy's social interaction at least when breaking windows. On March 4, 1931, the long-suffering Mr. Zookman (and it is surely him with the meat cleaver in the final panel) has his window broken again as Skippy and an unseen playmate warm up their arms with some practice throws. In the strip's second panel, the ball sails over the head of a leaping Skippy and in the third, as Mr. Zookman emerges in response to another broken window, Skippy implores to the thrower, "Get 'Em down." A single-panel episode on May 12, 1931, has Skippy running for it after breaking a shop window with the owner in hot pursuit. Skippy says, "Now I know I shoulda gone fishin'!" On August 15, 1931, as a shopkeeper chases him for breaking his window playing baseball, Skippy exclaims, "Gee! A guy's got to sow his wild oats sometime." A year later on August 15, 1932, in a single-panel episode, the shopkeeper stands in his store looking out through a broken window as a group of seven baseball-equipped boys run in various directions. Skippy says, ""Nothin' but broken glass all day! At this rate, we'll never get started." And on April 20, 1933, Skippy and another boy are playing Duck on the Rock and this results in a broken window; to which, Skippy says, "That's not Duck on the Rock! What will Mister Krausmeyer think?" All these instances take place on the streets in the company of other boys. By contrast on March 28, 1931, Skippy practices pitching and misses a target he has set up and breaks a window in his home. In the last panel, from his hiding spot in a trash can, he remarks, "that's what comes of bein' such a good pitcher that ya can't help throwin' curves." On February 24, 1932, he breaks a window while shooting arrows at a target and notes, "I'm getting a little nearer, anyway." On June 20, 1932, he breaks a window practicing his batting and when asked by his mother, "Well, what have you to say for this?" replies "I'll never make the team, battin like that." For this transgression he is sent to his room where he harrumphs, "Some home." On October 18, 1933, aiming a horseshoe at a stake he manages to let it go at a right angle smashing a window. The gag "Gee somebody must o' put a horse on it!" is a nice non-risqué double entendre pun. So while *Ginger Meggs,* with its larger number of panels to fill and greater expanse of story to tell, concentrated on social spaces, and the people within them, for broken window jokes, the daily *Skippy* strip could deliver stories in both social and domestic settings.

Crosby seldom used broken window gags in his Sunday strips. On January 3, 1932, he used the same set up of a pogo stick as his daily of December 29, 1925. In the 1932 instance, he used ten panels to set up Skippy crashing through a drug store window in the 11th. In those panels he moved Skippy from the second floor of his house to the streets and then through the window. All of these panels were speechless. In the final panel, through the smashed window, Skippy says, "A-A Ch-Chawklet Soda!" Crosby, like Bancks, worked the combination gag in his Sunday strip. Crosby's silent strip of Sunday, October 18, 1931, in which Skippy kicks a ball through a neighbor's window is a lesser effort with the only gag being his quick thinking to rush inside and get another toy to play with to misdirect suspicion when the neighbor glares over the fence. In one more instance, on May 7, 1933, he had a bored Skippy run after another boy who seemed in a rush to be somewhere. Skippy thought "must be a fire or somethin'," but the response was "I broke a window! Look in back of ya!" On doing so Skippy sees a cop in hot pursuit and decides to stop because he has done nothing. Nonetheless, the cop arrests Skippy. The 12 panels neatly worked three standards, the broken window, a play on the gag of anyone in a rush being asked where is the fire, and interactions with the police, a feature of many kid comics.

THE POLICE

In a 1938 strip, a boy whose father is a glazier tricks Ginger into breaking a shop window. Ginger says his prayers in the last panel asking, "if the police do find out will you make them believe that terrible awful boy tricked me into breaking that window."[5] Ginger was often worried about the police, but he also could use them for his own purposes. The police had a more frequent appearance in *Ginger Meggs* than in *Skippy*. From the context of the strips this difference appears to again be because of the greater space Bancks had to fill. In the third episode of Ginger Meggs on November 27, 1921, Gladys talks a policeman out of arresting Ginger and friends for borrowing a herd of goats for a race. On March 5, 1922, Ginger's Mum prevents a policeman from arresting him with a well-swung broom and leads Ginger away saying, "Them Pleece thinks they can do anything." On May 14, 1922, Ginger and his friends accidentally cause serious mayhem to a band practice with a giant bunger (a rather large firecracker). Nabbed by a policeman, Ginger is rescued when his friends drop a bunger under the cop, who, dazed and confused, in the next panel says, "its them Bolsheviks. One ov 'em musta threw a bomb." The following year, on January 14, 1923, an erstwhile citizen trying to help out Ginger, by gathering a cicada from a tree, manages to fall on a policeman. The policeman arrests the man and reads him his rights, "Remember now that everything you say will be taken down, altered and used as evidence against you." This irreverent attitude to the police, perhaps something to be expected in Sydney, was matched by a fear of police authority. So, for instance, on December 6, 1925, a policeman threatens Ginger with jail (gaol) after a misunderstanding. Ginger visibly sweats at this suggestion. The authority of the police though could also be mobilized for retribution against Ginger's nemesis Tiger Kelly as it was in the aforementioned broken window strip of November 2, 1924, in the concluding panel of which Ginger and Bennie watch with glee as a policeman hands out punishment to Tiger. On October 17, 1926; March 25, 1928; September 30, 1928; July 27, 1930; and February 5, 1933, Tiger Kelly again and again finds punishment at the hands of the police through Ginger's good luck or careful plans. Ginger was not above appealing to the good nature of one policeman, Mr. Brady, when he set out on February 9, 1930, to help his friend Raggsey retrieve money owed by Tiger Kelly. That Ginger wanted Raggsey to get his money so that he could buy Ginger an ice cream did not change the representation of the policeman as good-natured, or at least susceptible to Ginger's guile. And while Ginger could generally rely on Tiger to get in trouble with the police, on August 24, 1930, a new policeman in the process of arresting Kelly for a minor infraction involving Ginger discovers that Tiger is the son of his friend and lets him off. Here Banck's turned the expected joke, of the police catching Tiger and helping out Ginger, on itself.

Long-running comic strips generally set up stock situations in which the humor is not so much the situation as such, but the way in which it plays out. In *Krazy Kat*, for instance, George Herriman had Ignatz Mouse throw a brick at Krazy Kat and Offica Pup intervene. That description, which covers the vast majority of the strip over 30 years, both captures what happened in the strip and does it no justice whatsoever. The point is the way Herriman told the story in any given episode. In *Ginger Meggs*, Tiger receiving his comeuppance at the hands of the police became a standard theme of the strip. Banck's looked for new ways to work his humor, which included inversion. Sometimes a standard joke could be worked in to a familiar scenario. So for instance on January 6, 1929, Bancks had Tiger Kelly take a cigar from Ginger that Eddie Coogan had given him. When Tiger lit the cigar it exploded in his face and Ginger is able to laugh at his good fortune inadvertently caused by Coogan. Bancks reworked this joke three years later on February 28, 1932. Ginger buys an exploding cigar intent on having Tiger take it from him. In the midst of doing so, Tiger is interrupted by a policeman who he tries to buy-off with the cigar. When it duly explodes in his face the policeman roughs up Tiger before arresting him. Combining the exploding cigar joke and Tiger being apprehended by the police joke must have pleased Bancks considerably since he repeated it in 1938.[6]

Although the daily *Skippy* comic strips up to 1933 did not carry many episodes involving the police, there were some irreverent strips in the early years. On October 11, 1923, in *Life*, before the syndication of the daily *Skippy*, a playmate and Skippy conspire to topple a cop. In 14 unframed panels Crosby showed the ploy going wrong despite Skippy kneeling behind the cop. His friend lacks the gumption to shove the cop. Noticed by the cop, Skippy sweats great gobs before managing to hightail it and then visit his friend, baseball bat in hand, for a little chat. On September 22, 1925, having drilled holes in a fence to watch the baseball world series Skippy and friends are chased off by a cop, who then proceeds to peer through the hole himself. On May 25, 1926, Skippy faces the wrath of the policeman father of a competing suitor for a girl. On October 11, 1925, in his best cop gag Crosby has Skippy insult a policeman who gives chase. Skippy, breaking the fourth wall, says, "When they laid out the city they must o' knowed this was comin'." The cop catches up with Skippy hiding in a pipe and prepares to dose him with water, to which Skippy implores, "Oh Officer! And me scarsely more than a child." Thereafter, cop gags disappear from the daily *Skippy* comic strip for four years. On March 28, 1929, Skippy thinks he is passing fruit to an accomplice, but that friend has disappeared and instead an unimpressed cop looks down at the unaware Skippy. Then in 1929 Skippy becomes a part-time traffic cop for 16 episodes between June 4 and 22. By having Skippy become the cop Crosby added some freshness to rather tired jokes. For instance, the last episode of the series has Skippy refusing a bribe from a friend explaining, "Ya can't buy a cop with money. Not a nickel, anyway." That Skippy's beat is a mostly empty street and the infringer in a soap box cart is part of the charm. In an earlier episode on June 6 he tells a boy pulling a loaded soap box cart that there is "no heavy truckin' on this boulevard after eight A.M." When Skippy notices a car get stolen he tells the exasperated owner on his return that there was no time to ring an alarm, but that he did get the number of the car. And in another instance of car theft on June 18 he tells the owner that yes indeed he knows who stole it, but "I never tell tales out of school."

In these Skippy-as-cop strips, Crosby was still looking for the gag and if some social commentary was present that was more by accident than intent. But beginning in mid-August 1930 Crosby began a three-month-long series of strips directed at the corruption of Prohibition and at the rise of gangsters like Al Capone. This "Jacketeer" series of strips was certainly different from anything Bancks ever attempted. In these strips, which continued through to November 14, 1930, Crosby fundamentally altered the nature of *Skippy* moving it from a gag strip to an overly didactic melodrama. The sequence ended rather abruptly, possibly because of the reaction of readers and newspaper editors, or because Crosby had nowhere to take the story line. In any case, on November 15, 1930, he reverted to a gag strip. Soon enough Crosby's tone shifted and rather than dealing with crime and corruption as a serious issue he offered some gag cop strips. The first of these on January 23, 1931, has Skippy saw the top of his bed post off to use as a truncheon. The strip is a wordless two-panel episode with his mother discovering the altered bed in panel one and Skippy leaning on a street corner swinging his truncheon. On May 21, 1931, Skippy gets pinched for stealing fruit from a street display and says, "An' yet they call cops public servants." On more or less the same theme Crosby has Skippy running from a cop on June 15, 1932, and saying, "So! This is what we pay taxes for!"

Much of the humor in both Bancks's and Crosby's strips drew on the same vein of gags to be had from a cop walking the beat. One tried and true gag was the sentimental Irish cop with a love for music from the home country. Although the notion of the Irish policeman was far more established stereotype in the USA, and something far more likely to be encountered than in Australia, Bancks, not Crosby, deployed this gag. In a variation of the Ginger/Tiger/Cop scenario, Bancks had Ginger playing on the street to raise money for Ragsey (who had lost a g in his name since the previous year). Tiger, noticing this performance, tries to rough-up Ginger, but an appreciative crowd beat Tiger, who then hasten to find a policeman to report the unlicensed Ginger's busking. The cop duly breaks up the performance and carries Ginger off to the station, but on the way asks him to play "The Dear Little Shamrock." On completion of the song the cop lets Ginger off. Such gags stretched back to the nineteenth century and, for instance, *Life* magazine in its original incarnation as an illustrated humor magazine published a cartoon by Franklin Morris Howarth on October 20, 1892, with just this theme of the Irish cop being swayed from his duty by a song from the old country. Such gags said something about the power dynamics in large cities, but were more American than Australian in nature.[7] While Crosby tried to work fresh angles on jokes, such as having Skippy become a cop, Bancks tended to work more established veins of humor, and ones that were often drawn from America.

RACE

In 1992, I argued that as much as *Ginger Meggs* could be seen at various times in its history as capturing, in a symbolic form, aspects of Australian identity, the strips mediation of Australians' use of American culture played a role in its popularity and success.[8] Indeed, the first *Ginger Meggs* episode adapted a breaking a window gag that had appeared in a pre-1921 American comic strip *Toonerville Trolley*. In addition to the similarities between *Skippy* and *Ginger Meggs* that I have teased out so far, there are several other instances where the gags paralleled each other. For instance, at different times Skippy and Ginger both flipped coins to decide whether to indulge themselves, or do the right thing. Bancks had Ginger go through this motion on November 1, 1925, and then used the joke again April 26, 1942. Crosby had Skippy flip a coin to decide whether to go home or to the movies and keep tossing until he got his desired result on November 27, 1932, and then again on August 23, 1942. In both Bancks's and Crosby's case, the second version was a fresh drawing and not a reprint, but the joke was recycled with little variation, a not uncommon practice among comic strip artists. Ginger of course was not derivative of Skippy, but there were some broadly shared attitudes that both Bancks and Crosby drew on for gags.[9] But Bancks used more ethnic humor gags than Crosby and many of Bancks's gags used stock stereotypes more resonant of the USA than Australia. Ethnic humor was not the mainstay of either *Ginger Meggs* or *Skippy*, but the instances of Bancks using it were greater than Crosby. In *Ginger Meggs* ethnic humor was most commonly associated with Joe the Italian green grocer. In his first appearance in the ball through the window strip on April 30, 1922, Bancks's presentation relied on the then casual racial slur "dago." So when the ball goes through the Joe's window, Ginger's girlfriend Min feels sorry for "poor old Dago Joe." To which Ginger replies, "Dinkum Min that aint nothing ter 'im Gosh! Dagos as tons o munny I bet e don't care about that winder a bit." The usual defense of this sort of racial joke is that it simply reflects the times and to be sure one could hear similar sentiments commonly expressed in Australia well into the latter half of the twentieth century. Bancks worked a vein of racial humor that dated back at least to 1890 in Australia when *The Bulletin* magazine carried cartoons of Italian organ grinders as a means of mocking the import of foreign labor to Australia. *The Bulletin* was an important weekly that helped shape Australian identity, humor, republican politics, and an important comic art tradition. It was also virulently racist and had "Australia for the White Man" as a running header.[10] Bancks's *Ginger Meggs* drew on this tradition for better or worse and, for instance, his March 26, 1922, episode had an Italian organ grinder. But in this first appearance of Joe, it is perhaps worth noting that the sentiments portrayed are not necessarily Bancks's, but of Ginger and that Ginger is clearly wish projecting that Joe will not be concerned about the window. When speaking with Ginger's mother, Bancks had Joe show his growing Australianess by saying "By Crika" (crikey), a word that Steve "The Crocodile Hunter" Irwin would later deploy to distinguish himself as thoroughly Australian. Furthermore, understanding this racial dimension has to be tempered by Bancks situating this early version of Ginger Meggs as a more rough neck working-class kid and the strip's humor was on the whole less whimsical than in later years. Bancks's dialogue tries to capture this tone. All that said, the depiction not only reflected Australian culture of the day, but also reinforced it. Bancks reshaped his depiction of Joe in later years, so an episode of June 6, 1926, has Ginger and Joe on friendly terms. Likewise, on July 31, 1927, Joe lets Ginger slip out the back door of his shop so as to avoid a beating from Tiger Kelly. Joe is not any less stereotypical in these episodes, still sporting his large mustache and Italian Australian accent. But the stereotype has shifted from the aggressive dago to an avuncular ethnic. And while Joe was avuncular the Italian ice cream shop owner in an episode of June 1, 1930, remained caustic, albeit under provocation from Ginger and a friend innocently trying to pass a fake coin.

Bancks also deployed racial depictions of Chinese Australians. In the March 26, 1922, episode, with the Italian organ grinder, a large dog Ginger is trying to return to his owner tosses about a Chinese man pushing a cart laden with fruit. Dressed Western style and wearing a derby, the Chinese man when sitting on the ground with his smashed fruit all around him exclaims "whoffor" and perhaps what Bancks meant to be expletives in some fake Chinese characters. To make clear this is a Chinese purveyor of fruits, Bancks has the derby tossed off and the man revealed to have a queue. The use of the queue was a fairly typical way to connote the Chineseness of its wearer, but after the Xinhai Revolution of 1911 the hairstyle mostly disappeared. On the other hand, Bancks's depiction of a Chinese man selling fruits from a cart was not so far fetched. Many Chinese arrived in Australia as the result of a gold rush in the 1850s. Having been driven off the goldfields, many established themselves as market gardeners around the outskirts of Sydney producing crops that they sold in the market in Sydney and giving rise to a Chinatown around Dixon Street. Bancks had another Chinese selling fruits in an episode of March 11, 1923, and again when scuttled he said "whoffor" and indicating that he was indeed Chinese Australia "Oh Clickey whoffor" (again crikey). Whereas Bancks's representation of Italian Australians softened a little, his depiction of Chinese Australians seems to have hardened. In an episode of June 3, 1928, Bancks has Ginger accidentally, but unapologetically, break the window of Ah Kee's Laundry, to which the said proprietor appears in the next panel asking "Whaffor." And in this representation Bancks had him dressed in Chinese costume (or at least the artist's rendition of such) and wearing a queue. The premise of a Chinese laundry owes little to circumstances in Australia and much to those existing in the USA, or at least in New York.[11] Chinese laundries were almost certainly nonexistent in Australia. For instance, an official report on the contribution of the Chinese in the state of New South Wales, of which Sydney is the capital city, makes no mention of Chinese laundries, but does mention market gardening and fruit selling.[12]

Percy Crosby by and large avoided such race humor. The only overt instance in the dailies from 1925 to 1933 occurred on August 4, 1925, in which Skippy asks Sambo to play a game of catch. But Sambo is taking his father to be measured for a gold tooth for his birthday. The visuals are as racially charged as the name Sambo implies. The minstrel show origins of such jokes would have made them immediately familiar to Australians, who had, as the cultural historian Richard Waterhouse noted, been inordinately fond of such performances since 1838.[13] So on June 12, 1932, when Bancks deployed a figure straight out of minstrelsy in a white-black baby mix up he was not so much employing an American concept, but rather a predigested Australian take on minstrelsy even in the absence of African Americans who were the targets of such mockery. As awful as the representation of race is in these comics, Americans and Australians shared a vision of finding such instances humorous. In the case of minstrelsy jokes it scarcely matters that both Crosby and Bancks, as far as I can tell, used such a joke only once up to 1933, but that the joke was available to both of them. And the point here, for this work at least, is not so much that Crosby and Bancks at best had an easy acceptance of the racial humor of the day, but that by the 1920s there were well-established norms of popular culture that worked their way through kid comic strips on both sides of the Pacific.[14] Nowhere was this clearer than in the use of soap box and billy carts in *Skippy* and *Ginger Meggs*, respectively.

BOXES AND CARTS

From 1921 to 1933, at least 11 Ginger Meggs strips used a billy cart joke. From 1925 to 1933, 45 Skippy daily strips featured soap box carts. In Australia, the billy carts were called that because they owed their origin to carts pulled by goats, or billy goats. In the USA, the carts were built from soap boxes. In Australia, at least in latter years, wooden crates used for fruit and vegetables were a common building material.[15] Crosby's use of soap box cart jokes predated *Skippy* and featured a sled modified with a soap box as a carriage. The joke though about not hitting a stump and the owner of "the boat" not taking orders from free passengers was good enough to feature in a future *Skippy* strip on November 19, 1925. Banck's first cart joke occurred June 11, 1922, when Ginger who had been tasked with digging up the garden by his father sneaks off with his friend Bennie and drives the latter's cart down a hill loosing control and knocking several pedestrians head over heels before careening into a ladder knocking a painter through a window and upsetting his paint can on to the head of an unwary pedestrian. And of course the pedestrian is Ginger's father, who comments, "If this isn't just a bad dream, your troubles are only just about to begin." Two weeks later on June 25, 1922, Bancks had Ginger hitch up a cart to a goat and pick up Min. Ginger's arch rival let loose another goat and mayhem followed, resulting in the destruction of Ginger's cart after yet another out-of-control ride. Bancks then used goats as the brunt of jokes in strips in February and July 1923 before returning to a cart joke on September 5, 1926. In this episode, yet another out-of-control ride results in yet another broken window, but all is well since Ginger's brand new watch is not damaged. By 1926 then Bancks had figured that the out-of-control cart, and indeed the broken window, might simply be a mechanism for delivering another gag. Crosby too came to use the cart, not so much as the focus of the gag, but a delivery mechanism.

On April 6, 1926, Crosby had Skippy careening downhill in a soap box cart. Against common convention, the action in each panel moved from right to left. At first the cart's progress is reasonably slow and Skippy's companion asks him, "Don't ya just love this Skippy," to which he answers yes to, but wonders. And as the cart picks up speed in the second panel, depicted by more dramatic speed lines, Skippy's friend asks what he is wondering. The reply in the last panel, where the cart is moving at an extremely rapid pace signaled by wonky wheels and a perspective that shows greater vertical descent, is that he wonders "if that sewer's open." Concerns about an open sewer became a standard soap box cart joke for Crosby. A few weeks later on May 17, 1926, Skippy appeared as a passenger hanging on for dear life, and managing to cover the eyes of the driver, in a soap box cart that was already airborne in the first panel. In the second panel Skippy's derby blows off, so fast is the cart moving. The strip moves from left to right in the panels and the only dialogue is in the third panel when Skippy says, "Take it easy Eddie!" as the cart hits a rock and begins to disintegrate mid-air. On August 26, 1926, Crosby again used a soap box derby *mise-en-scène*. But in this strip, the three-panel action of the soap box as it moves from a stationary start in panel one to airborne speed in panel three is but a backdrop to the tale told by sometime supporting character Yacob. The story goes that one Mr. Schultz becomes so jealous of the extra soup Mr. Tootlebon receives from Yacob's Aunt Gussie that he refuses to join in the "guzoonhite" when the latter sneezes.

This strip gave Crosby a formula for soap box gags that he used on frequent occasions. So, for instance, on October 5, 1926, Yacob and Skippy again ride in a soap box cart in a three-panel strip. In this episode, the cart is somewhat fancier, complete with a side door and a horn. As the action picks up in the second panel the door flies open and the horn comes off; by the third panel the cart is airborne again, disintegrating and heading for a nose-dive. Crosby depicted all of this in a great flurry of lines and the final panel where the cart comes apart with bits flying all about reflects the gag. Yacob tells Skippy that the Zookmans (the unfortunate butcher of the broken window?) had dropped around for a visit. As his Uncle Louie saw it, the Zookmans could not have seen much of each other "'cause when Mr. Zookman ain't havein one o' his fits Mrs. Zookman havin' Saint Vitas dance." In another episode on October 18, 1920, Skippy's friend tells him about jumping fish seen on a trans-Atlantic immigrants' voyage. The punch line was that the fish jump to see if they are still in the gulf-stream.

Crosby had more variations than Bancks on the basic out of control down a hill gag that underpinned the soap box strips. As already noted snow and indeed ice allowed him to work the theme through other instances. Although it does snow in Australia and there are ski fields, the major centers of population rarely receive snow and certainly nothing that settles. On Sunday, December 28, 1930, Crosby had Skippy decide to one-handedly take on those occupying a snow fort. Skippy doses himself in water and then begins to roll down a hill. As he gathers speed, the snow clings to him and he becomes a giant human snow bolder that smashes through the fort. The final panel shows a bruised and bandaged Skippy in bed musing that folks have to get up early to get the best of him. On Sunday, January 19, 1936, Crosby showed Skippy's friends repeatedly pushing him in his cart up a hill, followed by him careening down it. The gag turned on this being training for football (Fig. 2.1)

Both Bancks and Crosby then created comic strips that extended the standard gag form that developed into layered narratives. Numerous

Fig. 2.1 *Skippy, Des Moines Register*, January 19, 1936

authors including Barbara Postema, Neil Cohn, Nick Sousanis, and Thierry Groensteen have written extensively on the dynamics of communication in comics, the manner of cognition and processes of narratology.[16] My purpose here is not to go into these various theoretical approaches, but some acknowledgment of the way both *Ginger Meggs* and *Skippy* developed and used conventions of comics art to tell their stories is important. These include, of course, the use of panels, word balloons, and a distinctive character. Beyond these features, both strips mostly used a left-to-right transition to relay the action and speed lines to depict motion. Such features were on the whole common to most comic strips. Both Bancks and Crosby developed the layered mechanism for delivering a joke. This mechanism used repetition, and sometimes even multilayered repetition, familiarity, and variation to create humor. Crosby's *Skippy* of December 16, 1926, is a useful case in point. Read by itself, the dialogue in the strip is rather straightforward. In panel one Skippy is asked if he believes in "Santy Claus". In panel two he says he does. The joke then seems topical because of the Santa reference in December. But then the punch line takes a turn with Skippy saying in the last panel, "But what good'll it do us if the sewer is open." The joke remains topical more or less, but its resolution is in the unexpected resort to another factor, the sewer, which trumps any importance given to Santa. The joke works even without reference to other episodes of *Skippy*, but gains resonance for the reader aware of the open sewer issue for Skippy's soap box cart adventures. Part of the joke lays in the repetition of the open sewer gag. In addition to one layer of repetition, there is the underpinning visual narrative structure for most of Crosby's cart jokes. In panel one the cart is stationary or picking up speed. In panel two the cart is airborne, but not precariously so as yet. And in panel three, chaos is at hand, or momentarily, since the cart has gathered a hellish speed. Explained like this, the joke does not seem funny (an explained joke seldom is) and the pleasure of this layer is in the telling, which is to say Crosby's art. This episode was the third time Crosby used the sewer joke and by no means the last. This aspect of repetition did more than provide a way to recycle jokes it created an overall narrative thematic for the strip, as did broken window gags. Crosby extended this theme in a 12-panel strip of Sunday, February 14, 1932. The strip opens with Skippy and a passenger in an already swiftly moving sled. Skippy advises his passenger to think carefully about purchasing Yacob's ice skates. As the sled picks up speed in each succeeding panel, Skippy ticks off a list of concerns from rust, to frayed straps, and so on. In the final panel, as the sled is about to hit an iced over pond, Skippy asks, "has anyone tried out the ice yet?" Although he has been building to this punch line, it remains unexpected because so often in the daily strip Crosby set the joke up less directly. In this strip, the reader is led to the punch line through Skippy's downhill soliloquy of the issue of Yacob's ice skates. For a strip like Crosby's that relied on gags, but did from time to time have longer narrative arcs, the repetition of joke-forms created a type of narrative that gave Skippy his character. Comics aficionados like Jerry Robinson and Jared Gardner often describe Skippy as "philosophical" and his concern about open sewers and that the ice might not yet be ready for his weight, were but some of the means that Skippy pondered the nature of life.

The episode of *Ginger Meggs* from January 31, 1932, had Ginger and his friend Bennie tasked with picking up a crate of chickens from the railroad station and transporting them to Mrs. Nelson. With a full page at his disposal, Bancks told the story over his usual 12 panels. In the first panel Bancks set the scene with Ginger and Bennie, accompanied by Mike and Tony, respectively, Ginger's dog and monkey, speed down a sidewalk on Ginger's billy cart. Along with the requisite speed lines, Bancks showed that Ginger was in motion by drawing his hair as being swept back so that Ginger's hair became an additional set of speed lines. Having received their instructions, Ginger and Bennie pick up the crate, and in the sixth panel the billy cart is out of control on a steep descent. In the seventh panel the bill cart crashes into a tree. Prior to this strip Bancks had used the crash as the ultimate panel and the one in which the gag was delivered. In this episode then he took his joke form – the billy cart – and altered his normal delivery of that over 12 panels, truncating it to seven panels. Bancks then used the other five panels to tell the joke that he had set up. While the convention in Western comics is to move action within a panel from left to right to match the reading direction Bancks generally varied the direction. By so doing, Bancks made it hard to read the strip at a glance. That is, while a reader will on the whole move through the strip left to right across the page and then loop back to the left to move down the page and read the next three panels left to right, it is also possible to take in a page at a glance. So, for instance, when conducting this research I could page through my research photographs of the strips and spot those with a billy cart without having to carefully read the whole strip. It seems fair enough to assume that a reader of the newspaper turning to the comics page would at first view the whole page, if only momentarily, before moving on to read it. Such a reader approaching this strip would notice at a glance the billy cart and a moment's more regard would have told the reader the expected crash does not occur in the last panel. The shifting direction of the panels makes scanning the comic difficult, and to understand the action a closer reading is required. Whether this was a deliberate strategy of Bancks's is uncertain. In this instance, the first seven panels are a set piece of a billy cart joke, but the last five offer a fresh joke. The chickens escape the smashed crate and Ginger and Bennie round them up from various yards, but worry since a black one seemed to have disappeared. The gag is that when they deliver the chickens to Mrs. Nelson there are nine but only six had been sent to her. Clearly, Ginger and Bennie had taken other people's chickens from their yards (Fig. 2.2)

Fig. 2.2 *Ginger Meggs, Sunday Sun*, January 31, 1932

Another example of Bancks's layering of his jokes occurred on October 2, 1932. His billy cart strip that day set up a final panel in which the joke did not derive directly from the mad careening downhill, but was nonetheless an outcome of that ride. Ginger shows off his new cart to his Mum, who dryly comments, "I'll have to watch out the Buick people don't try kidnapping you." Setting off from the top of the hill accompanied by his pets Ginger sets himself for "a bit of Malcolm Campbell stuff" referencing the English land speed record holder. Ginger duly hits a stump and with his pets becomes airborne flying toward and open house window. The next panel shows a corpulent gentleman enjoying a peaceful bath only to have Ginger et al. land on him in panel 11. The joke comes in the last panel when the very flustered man reports to the police being attacked by two or three boys and several animals with murderous intent. Bancks then used repetition across several of his 12 panels building up to a final denouement, but offering some sight gags and sarcasm in the process. In this way, he layered his humor so the billy cart as such was not the sole driver of an episode. This took a different form in the full-page Sunday comic strip than in the smaller daily strip versions of Crosby's *Skippy*. With more space to lay out his story, Bancks did not develop the economy of a three-panel repetitive form, but rather worked the repetitive joke like billy carts and broken windows.

CROSBY AS A SUNDAY STRIP ARTIST

Crosby used a soap box cart joke 46 more times in his daily strips from 1927 to 1933. Bancks did not use billy cart jokes with such frequency, again a difference between a daily strip and a Sunday strip. Examining primarily the daily version of *Skippy* and comparing it to the Sunday, *Ginger Meggs* has the advantage of displaying differences in mode between a daily and a Sunday strip, while at the same time pointing to commonalities in humor. Nonetheless, Crosby could fill the 12 panels of a Sunday strip. One of his favorite techniques in the Sunday form was to stretch a gag over 11 panels with the formal gag only coming in the last panel. On May 11, 1930, Crosby had Skippy scale a small mountain to pick the single flower atop. In the 12th panel, he presented it to his mother saying "For Mother's Day, Mama." Skippy's mother is delighted with the flower. The gag is not so much the formal punch line, but Skippy's incredible exertion to obtain a single flower. On April 5, 1932, Crosby again had Skippy ascend a small mountain setting up a punch line of "I'm darned if I see any panorama." Fitting enough as this line was the gag was in the effort to climb. Crosby was adept at stretching a verbal gag too by filling time with visuals. On January 5, 1930, he had Skippy tell Yacob about word association mental tests in the first panel. In the second, Skippy starts with the word "baseball." Yacob does not respond with "bat" until the 11th panel. In the meantime, day has turned to night and Skippy has gone home had dinner, listened to a radio serial, and then returned for the answer. In the final panel, he says to Yacob, "You win." Crosby also stretched out time on April 6, 1930. The first three panels show Skippy and a friend sitting wordlessly on a curb. In panel four, Skippy asks, "Do you like eggs?" To which the friend replies, "uh," in the fifth panel. Three more wordless panels follow before Skippy asks, "How? Fried?" In the tenth panel the friend answers, "uh." The joke picks up pace in the 11th panel when Skippy says he has to go, but will meet again the next day. In the final panel Skippy reflects, "It isn't everyone you can sit down with by the hour and bat our a little chatter." These gags would not have worked in the daily strip because Crosby needed the space to stretch out the pace, which only Sunday's version allowed him. Crosby's control of the form can been seen in two contrasting strips of June 15, 1930, and August 10, 1930, in which he played with common place truism that no one wants to go to the dentist and that when you need a doctor one tends to have an immediate need. On June 15, Skippy whiles away his time by watching a trench being dug, observing some furniture removalists at work, doing some window shopping, balancing on a railing, and even reading before arriving late at the dentist and so having to forgo his appointment. Again Crosby holds off all dialogue until the final panel and the pleasure of the joke is somewhat the anticipation of where Crosby is taking the reader. On August 20, and somewhat unusually for the Sunday episodes, Skippy is moving at a great pace, vaulting one handed over a fence, hoofing it up a hill, and descending on foot at so great a pace he clips a rock and takes a spill but recovers to pound up steps to a doctor's office. He tells the doctor that his Papa wants him to come quick because "our cellar door's stuck." Somewhat nonplussed the doctor asks, "what does he want me to do about it?" To which Skippy replies in the last panel, "I don't know, but Papa's finger is stuck in it." This gag could have worked in a three- or four-panel daily, but the extra space gave Crosby a longer set up, heightening anticipation, and making the punch line all the sweeter. The humor too was universal because the cellar door could have been any door anywhere in the world. It is such a good joke it is surprising not to have seen it replicated elsewhere.

Ginger Meggs and *Skippy* were two distinct comic strips that worked similar veins of humor. The key difference between the two as I have shown was mostly that between a daily strip and a Sunday strip rather than any reflection of the different scope and scale of Australian and American culture. At the same time though, this is not to suggest that each and every joke in the strips was available to readers in both countries. In particular, the language in some of the early *Ginger Meggs* strips required a working knowledge of the Australian idiom, and some familiarity with the patois of Italian Australians. Climate too played a role, giving Crosby a winter palette to work with, which Bancks lacked. The fate of both artists was somewhat tragic. Crosby locked in a mental institute in 1948 after suffering a mental breakdown and never again able to produce his strip. Bancks died suddenly aged 63 in 1952. Skippy vanished with his creator, but Ginger Meggs lives on now in the hands of an East Village, New York City–based Australian.

NOTES

1 New York, 1870, https://www.census.gov/population/www/documenta
tion/twps0027/tab10.txt; New York, 1900, https://www.census.gov/
population/www/documentation/twps0027/tab13.txt; Sydney: Norman
Abjorensen, and James C. Docherty, *Historical Dictionary of Australia*
(Lantham: Rowman & Littlefield, 2014), 432.

2. Ian Gordon, "The Symbol of a Nation: Ginger Meggs and Australian
National Identity," *Journal of Australian Studies*, Vol. 16, No. 34
(September 1992): 1–14.

3. Jared Gardner, "Introduction," *Skippy Volume 1: Complete Dailies 1925–1927*
(San Diego: IDW Publishing, 2012), 7–58.

4. Tyler Anbinder, *Five Points: The Nineteenth-Century New York City
Neighborhood* (New York: Free Press, 2001), 376.

5. James Bancks, *More Adventures of Ginger Meggs* (Sydney: Associated
Newspapers, 1939). Unfortunately I was unable to date this strip during
research at the State Library of NSW in 1987 and again in 2015.

6. The 1938 strip "Bang Goes a Cigar," was reprinted in James Bancks, *More
Adventures of Ginger Meggs* (Sydney: Associated Newspapers, 1939).
Unfortunately I was unable to date this strip during research at the State
Library of NSW in 1987 and again in 2015.

7. I made this point in *Comic Strips and Consumer Culture* (Washington, DC:
Smithsonian Institution Press, 1998), 18–20.

8. Ian Gordon, "The Symbol of a Nation."

9. In 1987 the late James Kemsley, then the artist producing *Ginger Meggs*, drew my attention to this shared tossing the coin gag. Kemsley and Jim Russell, the longtime artist on the other outstanding Australian comic strip *The Potts*, suggested that *Skippy* was a source of inspiration for Bancks. Just what they meant by inspiration was unclear, but Russell did point out that another Australian artist, Syd Nicholls, directly based the look of Sease, one of the supporting characters in his *Fatty Finn* comic strip, on Skippy using the beat up derby and a similar tie. This conversation took place in the Sutton Grove Hotel May 20, 1987, and as with any story told in an Australian pub should be treated with some caution. But the *Fatty Finn* strip of February 14, 1932 (yet another broken window gag) clearly shows Sease is based on Skippy.

10. Stefanie Affeldt, *Consuming Whiteness: Australian Racism and the "White Sugar" Campaign* (Berlin: Lit, 2014), 214. On *The Bulletin* see Sylvia Lawson, *The Archibald Paradox: A Strange Case of Authorship* (Ringwood, VIC: Allen Lane, 1983).

11. For the development of Chinese laundries in the USA and the resulting popular stereotype, see John Kuo Wei Tchen, *New York Before Chinatown: Orientalism and the shaping of American culture, 1776–1882* (Baltimore: Johns Hopkins University Press, 1999).

12. Michael Williams, *Chinese Settlement in NSW: A Thematic History* (Sydney: NSW Office of the Environment and Heritage, 1999), 20, https://www.environment.nsw.gov.au/resources/ . . . /chinesehistory.pdf

13. Richard Waterhouse, "The Minstrel Show and Australian Culture," *Journal of Popular Culture*, Vol. 24 (Winter 1990): 147–166.

14. At least three Sunday strips by Crosby used tar as a gag. Crosby did not attempt a race joke in any of these strips, which appeared April 13 and June 29, 1930, and April 17, 1932. Given that tar was so often used to make racial jokes, and given the absence of any other race jokes in the strips I have reviewed, Crosby might have had a change of mindset. But just as a single racist joke doesn't make someone a virulent racist, nor does the absence of such jokes make them not a racist, or indeed antiracist.

15. As a primary school student in Sydney, my neighbor built a cart from old vegetable crates for me to drive in my school's billy cart derby.

16. Barbara Postema, *Narrative Structure in Comics: Making Sense of Fragments* (Rochester, NY: RIT Press, 2013); Neil Cohn, *The Visual Language of Comics: Introduction to the Structure and Cognition of Sequential Images* (New York: Bloomsbury, 2014); Nick Sousanis, *Unflattening* (Cambridge, MA: Harvard University Press, 2015); and Thierry Groensteen, *The System of Comics* (Jackson: University Press of Mississippi, 2007) and *Comics and Narration* (Jackson: University Press of Mississippi, 2015).

CHAPTER 3

America and France: Perry Winkle and *Bicot*

Abstract This chapter examines what happened when an American comic was translated into French. It notes what was lost and added in translation. It points to the way that translating the words of a medium that mixes words and images to create meaning leaves traces of that original meaning in the images. In this and other ways, *Bicot* could be both French and American at the same time.

Keywords Martin Branner · *Bicot* · Perry Winkle · Race · Representation · Translation · Glocalization · France · Stereotypes · Domesticated

The American comic strip *Winnie Winkle* by Martin Branner, which first appeared in the New York *Daily News* and the *Chicago Tribune* September 21, 1920, is a particularly useful comic for examining the similarities and differences in the genre of kid's strips internationally. The strip had both a daily and Sunday version. The title character, Winnie, was a working girl and the strip commenced its run shortly after the passage of the nineteenth amendment to the US Constitution, which gave women voting rights, and dealt with changing social mores and many issues confronting women. Nonetheless, Branner relied on jokes about feminine artifice and pretensions for a great deal of the humor in the first decades of the strip. As a working-class young woman, Winnie aspired to improve her class position and strove for social betterment through depicting a refined modern self

© The Author(s) 2016
I. Gordon, *Kid Comic Strips*, Palgrave Studies in Comics
and Graphic Novels, DOI 10.1057/978-1-137-55580-9_3

both in manners and in dress. Through such behavioral changes, Winnie hoped to mix with a higher-class circle and attract an appropriate suitor. Winnie, who was in her late teens or early 20s, had a much younger adopted brother Perry. Throughout the 1920s, Branner turned over the Sunday page of the strip almost exclusively to the antics of Perry and his friends the "Rinkeydinks." Although Branner made Perry's antics the focus of the Sunday panels, he tied this to his overall theme by having Winnie constantly trying to curtail Perry's behavior and call him to order. Winnie was often publicly embarrassed by Perry's preference for running with the neighborhood kids rather than mix with the upper-middle-class types that Winnie wished him to make playmates.

In March 1923, the Paris-based daily newspaper *Excelsior*, owned by Paul Dupuy, began a Sunday supplement in an effort to boost circulation. This paper *Excelsior Dimanche* ran to around 16 pages and the first issue carried a Perry Winkle Sunday strip under the title *Bicot*. By the time Dupuy renamed the newspaper *Le Dimanche Illustré* the following March Perry had been joined by a version of another Chicago *Tribune* strip *The Gumps*, translated as *La famille Mirliton*, literally the Kazoo Family. Just why Dupuy chose to run these strips is unclear. Dupuy had been a frequent visitor to the United States and indeed in 1908 married Helen Browne of New York. Dupuy was a member of the French Parliament and his knowledge of the USA was such that in 1925 he was part of the official French mission to America led by Joseph Caillaux to negotiate the matter of allied debt from World War I. From accounts of Dupuy's early trips to the USA, undertaken for his father's newspaper the *Petit Parisien*, he purchased print machinery for the newspaper and it seems likely he met newspaper proprietors like his contemporary Joseph Medill Patterson of the *Chicago Tribune* and New York *Daily News*.[1] The appearance of French versions of these American comic strips then rested on existing trans-Atlantic connections and transactions, but more importantly on Dupuy's belief that the humor would translate. The newspaper flourished, reaching a circulation of 230,000 by about 1924. The Paris-issued paper continued to May 26, 1940, and a Vichy France edition appeared in Marseille from November 1940 to May 1944, the latter presumably without Bicot comic strips.[2]

Comparing the American Perry Winkle episodes with the reworked French-version strips offers useful points of contrast between American humor and French humor. Moreover, it provides a useful way to examine the different cultural contexts shaping the sort of humor derived from the activities of kids. For instance, *Bicot* translates to English as "wog." In recent years, the term arabo (arab) has been generally used to explain the title *Bicot,* but the less anachronistic translation along these lines would have been "street arab." The American *Webster*'s dictionary describes this term as "dated" and meaning "a homeless vagabond in the streets of a city and especially an outcast boy or girl: gamin." The *OED* suggests: "homeless child or young person living on the streets." But Perry had a home, a sister, and parents. His family was from the respectable working class, able to afford a radio if somewhat precariously on time payment, and aspiring to move into the middle classes. That Perry played with his friends in the streets, despite coming from a slightly better-off family, and one with middle-class aspirations, worked a particular vein of kid comic strip humor. In earlier kids strips from Wilhelm Busch's *Max und Moritz,* Rudolph Dirks's *Katzenjammer Kids,* to Richard Outcault's *Yellow Kid* and *Buster Brown* the core aspect of the humor centered on the contrast between prevailing notions of childhood innocence and the reality of the mischievous child. Outcault's *Buster Brown* offered a version of this humor in which the most refined-looking upper-middle-class child deliberately engaged in pranks and the like that upset adult decorum and accepted norms of childhood behavior. The humor relied on the recognition that the norms bore no relationship to reality. Branner's innovation in his Perry Winkle strips was to work the larger social drama of Winnie Winkle's class aspirations into a kid strip by placing Perry between his sister's hankering for respectability and the pull of his less well-off friends. The use of *Bicot* as the title of the strip, and as the French name for Perry suggests that the strip did not on the surface meet French expectations for this sort of "kid in the street" humor. At the very least the title *Bicot* had to signal the sort of humor to be expected. In the American version, Perry had few of the characteristics associated with the word *bicot.* To be sure, the strip in part relied on the sort of jokes to be had from kids playing in the streets, but much of the way it played out was in the seeming incongruity of someone dressed like Perry playing with his ill-dressed friends. This visual component of the strip formed an underpinning structure on which Branner could create a variety of humorous narratives. Titling the strip *Bicot* was but one way in which the French version reworked the verbal narrative to create a strip that would appeal in France. This chapter unpacks these differences by comparing episodes from the American strip with the translated French counterpart.

RACE

An immediate distinguishing feature of the Perry Winkle and the Rinkeydinks strips is the presence of a Chinese boy, "Chink," as one of the four stalwarts of the club in addition to Perry, Spud, and Pike. In the French version, these four are in turn Ernest, Bicot, Auguste, and Julot.[3] Naming a Chinese character Chink is of course racially epithet and offensive. Nonetheless, the character plays out in ways more complex than the reductive stereotype that such an offensive name suggests will follow. Examining some episodes where race is not necessarily central to the plot helps understand the place of Chink/Ernest in the strip. Many of the Perry/Bicot strips had seemingly relatively minor changes in the dialogue, but what might at first seem minor reveals some distinctive cultural differences. For instance, the episode published on February 3, 1924, in the USA and March 2 in France depicted Perry/Bicot's infatuation with Dorothy and his desire to purchase her a birthday gift. In both the versions, the episode plays out over 12 standard panels in a three by four layout with a single header panel. The header panel is the only panel that differs visually with the American version showing Perry's heart breaking as he gazes upon a disdainful Dorothy, with the heart appearing symbolically outside Perry's body with motion lines and onomatopoeia showing it cracking. Both Perry and Dorothy appear in full-body shots next to the Winnie Winkle title. In the French version, the header panel contains headshots of Bicot and Dorothée with the strips title *Bicot, président de club*, and the episode title *"La Fête de Dorothée"* [Dorothy's Birthday]. In French, rather than being president of the Rinkeydinks (rinky-dink means small and shoddy), Bicot was the president of *Le Club des Rantanplan*, the latter word an onomatopoeic for the sound of rolling drums that seems to have come from nursery rhymes, and then morphed in the 1960s into a Franco-Belgian comics dog character.[4] In the first panel of the strip, Winnie, Suzy in the French version, scolds Perry/Bicot for asking for a greater sum of money than she has given him. Both versions are similar enough. But Perry's reply in English that, "I knew darn well I wouldn't get it from a piker like you" proved untranslatable and was rendered as "je me souviendrai de ta génerosite" [I will remember your generosity]. This inability to translate the term piker shifts Perry's response from a direct statement of disappointment to a more sarcastic comment in the mouth of Bicot. In both the versions, Perry/Bicot wants to buy Dorothy a bottle of perfume, but lacking the necessary funds he persuades his fellow Rinkeydinks that they should combine their funds and purchase something special. The boys then argue over who should present the present to Dorothy and settle the matter with a series of coin tosses. In the American version of the strip, after losing a coin toss Chink says to Spike who is tossing the coin, "Do it over again an' let **me** toss it!! I dare ya!" These words are entirely absent from the French version. In both the versions the boys fight, the bottle breaks, and Dorothy is presented with her gift broken on the sidewalk. The strip published the following week on February 10, 1924, again saw Perry pursuing Dorothy, and again dealing with the rest of the Rinkeydinks. Perry manages to see off another boy who is talking with Dorothy by letting loose a cat that the boy's dog chases. He then takes Dorothy for chocolate ice cream sodas, to the amazement of the Rinkeydinks who are unaware of his cat trick. In the French version published on March 16, 1924, the action is very similar with some small exceptions. So Ernest, instead of saying as he does in the American version "an' I'm getting' sick an' tired of girls anyway!!," says in the French saying, "Moi, je suis fatigue de ses caprices!" [I am tired of her whims]. And in the French version, instead of buying sodas, Bicot buys himself and Dorothée ice cream, coffee, and cakes (Fig. 3.1).

At first glance, the different versions of these two strips might seem to have only minor variations dictated by dissimilar manners of expression between English and French. But the absence of Chink's stern words to Spike might signal several things. To be sure the panel in which they appeared was a busy panel with several word balloons and Chink's words were not central to setting up the joke. The words could easily have been removed to make the panel and the narrative flow smoother. In some ways then the question is not why the French translators and editors of the strip removed them, but why Branner included them. Despite the racial epithet, Chink is the equal of all the Rinkeydinks. His manner of speech is no different from the others and Branner drew him as a lanky character and, at least in the strips I have read, without any racial stereotyping. That is Chink, although drawn by Branner in a cartoon manner, is no more a caricature than the other characters. Importantly in all the instances I have seen in color, Chink's skin tone is pink and not the sort

Fig. 3.1   *Bicot, Dimanche Illustré*, March 16, 1924

of harsh yellow often used to represent Chinese in comics. His challenge to Spike then demonstrates their equality, or at least Chink's willingness to claim such status. Whether or not the absence of his words in the French versions displays something more than a desire to have a clearer panel is difficult to tell, but in this small way Chink's position in the club is somewhat lessened. Despite this omission of Chink's word balloon in his translation to Ernest in the March 2 strip, it is Ernest who offers in the French episode of March 16 the mature world-weary phrase of being "tired of her whims," rather than the more boyish American expression of being done with girls. The French episode of March 16 had one more example suggesting a different sensibility in kid strips and perhaps beyond. The children in the strip are of an indeterminate age, but seemingly no older than ten. Drinking coffee at that age seems precocious. At very least, this instance seems an important mark of the cultural differences between the versions with the French adaptation playing to a slightly more mature view of childhood. And Ernest at least in one episode displaying such a sensibility.

The place of Chink/Ernest in the two versions of the comic strip is not entirely clear. Beyond his name in the American version there was no effort at using him for a figure of racial humor. To be sure there were Chinese populations in both New York, where Branner lived, and Paris in the 1920s, but these were not particularly large populations. The Chinese in New York though were the subject of media fascination, perhaps best captured in Herbert Asbury's 1927 book *Gangs of New York* with its breathless dramatization of the career of the Hip Sing Tong leader Sai Wing Mock (best remembered as Mock Duck). And indeed Chinatown in Manhattan was the site of gawker tourism at the turn of the twentieth century. But in 1920 the total Asian population of New York City was just under 8,000.[5] There were far fewer Chinese living in Paris, indeed only around 2,000 by 1936, although in the 1920s these included such later well-known figures as Zhou Enlai and Deng Xiaoping.[6] The French version of course followed the American version in visuals and without the racial epithet "Chink" it may well be that Ernest was not so obviously Chinese to French readers.

Issues of race are put into a much sharper perspective in strips that deal with those of African origin. In an episode published April 20, 1924, in America, and June 29 the same year in France, Winnie makes Perry wear a fancy "imported suit from Paris" for Easter Sunday. Perry quickly offloads it on Spud, who in turn passes it to Spike and he on to Chink. Chink then waylays a boy of African descent "Sassafras" and tells him to swap cloths. Sassafras replies in the language of minstrelsy " Lawsy misto' chink dat suit too hifallutin' fo' me!" Branner also drew Sassafras as a blackface caricature. In the French version, Suzy simply tells Bicot that the new suit fits him perfectly. Bicot complains that it is a suit for a little girl and will dishonor him, which says something about how the French viewed American notions of Parisian fashion. The same scenario plays out with the suit moving from Bicot to Auguste, Auguste to Julot, and Julot to Ernest. Ernest then unloads it on Mamadou. None of these panels is altered except for the word balloons. Mamadou is the self same blackface caricature, and indeed in the French version he appears in the title panel. Mamadou though is a West African name and not some minstrelsy invention like "Sassafras." Like the Chinese in France, West Africans arrived during World War I. According to historian Joe Lunn, some 140,000 West Africans "served as combatants on the Western Front" as part of the French Army.[7] Despite the genuine name, the West African history of defending France, the character, and his equally stereotypically drawn mother show that race humor directed at those of African origins played universally. The episode also demonstrated something of a racial hierarchy in Branner's mind with the next to last recipient of the suit in its declension being Ernest and then Mamadou. The historian Wen Shuang in her 2015 PhD discussed the manner in which the French brought Chinese and Arab subalterns to Europe during World War I and the mutual antagonisms these two groups felt.[8] Branner's American humor in this episode perhaps unknowingly (or perhaps not given that he served in France in World War 1) played to this discomfort.

The French version occasionally displayed slightly different attitudes about race than the American strip. So, for instance, the episode of February 22, 1925, has Perry and the Rinkeydinks deciding to throw snowballs at a target. They ask Mose, an African American boy, "Hey Mose, wlll ya lend us that ol' hat for a target? We'll let you stand outside an' pick it up every time we knock it off'en th' fence!!" The French version published in *Dimanche Illustré* March 3, 1925, had the boys offer Moise an opportunity to earn money rather than the pleasure of simply being let to stand and pick up the hat. It is a small difference because the language of Mose/Moise, and indeed the name, was just as stereotyped. Perhaps the French translator could not believe that white boys might think allowing an African American boy to play with them was reward enough for his efforts.

CLASS AND GENDER

The American version of the strip was far more concerned with Winnie's class aspirations, or pretensions, than the French version. So, for instance, in the January 14, 1923, strip Winnie visits Jane, a young society woman, who has two tickets to a lecture on "The Cosmic Urge." But since her "Grandfawthaw" is alone she feels she "cawn't" attend. Winnie volunteers Perry to take the grandfather to the Park in a wheelchair so that she and Jane can attend the lecture. Perry, who wants to be out raising money for his club, seizes an opportunity when the old man falls asleep to put a "Please Help the Blind" sign on him and receives several donations.

The caper comes unstuck when Jane and Winnie happen on them in the park. Perry runs for home and takes refuge on the roof. The strip's main gag is having the well-to-do grandfather put in a position of a beggar to serve Perry's need. But Branner worked in his long-running theme of poking fun at Winnie's desire for middle-class respectability. The "Gradfawthaw" and the "cawn't" are the signs of Jane's class status and indeed suggest something rather higher than middle class. This element of humor, a sly satire on class aspirations, did not appear in the French version of March 11, 1923, in which "grandfawthaw" became the rather mundane "grand pere." In the French version, Suzy's friend Josephine (Jane) has tickets for a variety show and not a lecture. These social class–based jokes also occur in the February 4, 1923, American strip when Perry offers his services to a middle-class gentleman to clear his steps and sidewalk of snow. The language used displays class and class ideology. Impressed, because Perry "talks like a businessman" and is a "straightforward energetic little chap," the gentleman hires him and pays in advance. Perry then tells his father to do the work since he has the money in hand. The notoriously lazy Rip Winkle begins to chase after Perry but is stopped from doing so by the gentleman and his dog. Winnie comes across her father shoveling snow and exclaims "Fawthaw." In the French version published March 18, 1923, the gentleman's language lacks the appreciation for Bicot's business-like behavior and language and he simply hands over his money. And Winnie has no class aspirations in her voice, instead simply saying Papa when she sees him shoveling. These instances are fine-grained differences but ones worth examining.

One reason that the French versions of the strip elided the language of class was because Branner relied on the daily strips in the American version to build a reader's familiarity with Winnie's character so that this sort of underlying joke was understood with no need for a set up and delivery of a punch line. The daily strips also much more clearly showed the working-class position of the Winkle family, whereas the Sunday strips sometimes were not as immediately readable in that fashion. Despite being under financial constraints in the daily strips during the 1920s, Winnie often appeared in the Sunday comic strips dressed in haute couture seeded gowns. In a sense, Winnie's class aspiration was a form of situation comedy. This aspect was mostly absent from the French version because *Excelsior Dimanche* only carried the Sunday strip focusing on Perry. Another reason for this absence was that the sort of class aspirations Winnie exhibited were more grounded in American society and culture in the 1920s than they would have been in France. Unlike the United States, which saw the development of a new middle class in the 1920s, such a class did not develop in France until the mid-1960s. To be sure, the post–World War I experience in France was one of social change, but not of the scope and dimension of the USA.[9] Furthermore, Winnie as the strip's subtitle emphasized was a working girl and the notion of a shop assistant or office worker aspiring to middle-class status would have seemed odd in France, except perhaps through marriage, during the 1920s. Winnie was not uninterested in moving up through marriage, but she also constantly tried to do so by mingling with women of the middle class. Branner's strip was in part a response to the enfranchisement of women in the USA after the passage of the Nineteenth Amendment to the US Constitution. Women in France did not achieve enfranchisment until 1944. Branner also found the humor to be had from Winnie and Jane attending a lecture on "The Cosmic Urge," the sort of thing that the American New Woman of the era might have been expected to do, but on the evidence of this episode of *Bicot* not her French counterpart.[10]

This issue of class mobility had a gender tinge in the USA. Branner' satire of Winnie's aspirations was somewhat gentle and Branner had been a vaudeville dancer and through his comic strip acquired some middle-class respectability, in the way that money brought such status in the USA. Nonetheless, Branner's strip showed him to be highly ambivalent about Winnie's aspirations and this it seemed was because of her gender. In the February 4, 1923, strip Branner has Perry and Rip's client express admiration for what he takes as the drive for success and willingness to work hard of Perry. To be sure he was mistaken, but Branner here expressed the lifting oneself up by the bootstraps ideology of the Horatio Alger stories, something that of course Branner himself was in the process of doing.[11] Indeed his Sunday strips drew some of their humor from how hard Perry worked at not working hard. Again from the evidence of the French version of March 18, 1923, this language of self-improvement did not resonate with the French.

The strips in *Dimanche Illustré* showed many instances where an American situation did not translate so well into a French circumstance. For instance in a strip of March 18, 1923, Perry's mother calls to Rip Winkle to take the rug out and beat it. In the French version of May 13, the line instead becomes "Marie, please bring the rug out to the court-yard to be beaten." Marie is unseen in the strip in this or any episode, but clearly the notion of Rip taking the rug out did not seem appropriate to the French translator. Moreover, the translator seems to have missed that the Winkle family was not of a class that could employ a maid; the request to Marie seems to imply a domestic servant helping with household chores, which suggests that the sort of consumer lifestyle enjoyed by a comic strip working-class American family seemed the stuff of the French middle class.

BASEBALL

Although baseball has now spread to many countries, in the 1920s it was quintessentially American – at least as far as Europeans were concerned. The former pitcher and sporting goods entrepreneur Albert Spalding had toured Europe in 1889 and sporadic attempts had been made to get the game going in France. World War I certainly saw the game played more, but in general talented French sportsmen did not take it up.[12] Surprisingly, *Dimanche Illustré* published the Perry Winkle strips that featured baseball. So for instance, a strip of May 6, 1923, appeared in French on June 17 that year. The joke in the strip centered on Algernon Manypenny, who from his portly manner and gag name was clearly some well-to-do child whose parents Winnie wished to impress. Having arranged uniforms for the Rinkeydinks, Manypenny insists on being the pitcher for the team. Perry refuses and Manypenny takes back the uniforms. In the French version, rather than being Manypenny he becomes Grossac, literally Big Bag, a direct reference to his physical state rather than his wealth. And rather than insisting on being the pitcher Grossac wanted to be the team captain. The word play of Manypenny may not have been possible in French, but the switch from pitcher to captain suggests that baseball was not well understood in France and so the prestige of being pitcher had to be shifted to the more readily understood captain. Branner again emphasized the importance of the pitcher to a team, or at least Perry's desire to be well regarded as a pitcher, on September 16, 1923. In the French version of October 28, the issue becomes Bicot's Presidency of the Rantanplan Club rather than his position as pitcher. And it, yet another instance the episode of *Bicot* that appeared on July 27, 1924, had a panel redrawn to remove references in the original of May 18, 1924, to the baseball game being in the ninth innings and instead simply conveyed that the score was tied on two all. And when an opponent hit a winning home run in the bottom of the ninth instead of spectators exclaiming "home run" and Perry saying "Gee," Bicot conveys all the meaning saying, "we're finished."

Having lost the game in the May 18 episode, Perry and the Rinkeydinks return to play the next week minus the uniforms they lost as part of the bet on the game they had with their opponents the Gashouse Goofers. In this May 25 episode, Perry and the Rinkeydinks are astounded to see an African American boy ask to play while wearing one of the suits they lost the previous week. They take the suit from him, but he returns wearing another, and following another confiscation comes back in a third. The Rinkeydinks then follow him to the basement where he found the suits, but the Gashouse Goofers are laying in wait for the African American boy and the Rinkeydinks share in the beating they hand out. The French version of this strip appeared on October 12, 1924. It is unclear why, but it fell out of sequence with the series of strips that focused on the uniform saga of the Rinkeydinks in the American version. In America, the strip appeared the next week and led on to several other strips in which the Rinkeydinks attempted to retrieve their uniforms. These were either not used or fell out of order in France. Possibly the strip arrived late in France and could not be used earlier, or the French editors were uncertain how to translate it for their audience. In the American version the African American boy calls himself Sambo. In the French he is unnamed. But the French version works the joke in a different way. In the American version, as the Rinkeydinks descend to the basement, Branner's use of eyes against a black background shows the presence of the Gashouse Goofers. The word balloon indicating dialogue from within, "Shhh! Here comes de guy wot's been swipin' our ball suits! Don't make no noise!!!" makes it clear that the Goofers thinks the African American boy has been swiping their suits and that he is inadvertently leading the Rinkeydinks to a beating. In the French version the word balloon says, "Don't make a sound. The white kids come for their uniforms." This caption then changes the intent of Branner's joke making those inside African in origin and the beating the Rinkeydinks are about to receive intended. This shift in the way the joke plays out then relies on a move from the lazy carefree stereotype of Sambo to an image of more dangerous figures laying in wait to commit premeditated violence. Moreover, if a reader had been following the uniform saga such as it appeared in France, this October 12 strip made it seem like the African American boys had stolen the uniforms. In all of this it seems that it was easier for the French version of the comic strip to use race, or more specifically African origins, as a basis for humor, than baseball. Nonetheless, strips featuring baseball appeared regularly in *Dimanche Illustré* until the last Bicot episode on May 26, 1940, in the last edition of the paper shortly before the capitulation of France to the Germans in World War II.

FRANCE OR AMERICA?

The aforementioned suit joke of April and June 1924 and the transformation of the American Sassafras into Mamadou in the French suggests an issue of uncertainty as to where *Dimanche Illustré* wanted its readers to think the Bicot version of the strip was located. On the one hand the strip had the club playing baseball, but on the other several things were altered to make the strip more French in character. Some of these differences were rather minor, but telling for just that reason; that is, something clearly was at work that required some effort in localizing the strip despite its obvious American *mise-en-scène*. For instance, in the April 5, 1925, episode, translated from the March 29 American appearance, Bicot and the boys try to play an April Fool's Day gag using an old wallet left on the sidewalk. A hobo wise to their trick ignores it, but a well-to-do gentleman decides to reverse the prank by pretending to find money in the wallet. When he does so, the hobo grabs the wallet from him and runs off with the boys in chase. Stopped by a policeman, the hobo gives up the wallet to the boys who rejoice at getting the money before the gentleman arrives in the last panel to reclaim it. In the American version, the gentleman slips five dollars into the "pocket-book" and the boys think about getting a soda with the money. In the French version the amount is 20 francs and they think of going to the patisserie. But two other differences are far more noticeable. First the hobo is depicted as having a dark complexion. This does not play out in any fashion verbally, but is an important difference from the American strip that simply presented him in the same color tone as the boys. More tellingly though the policeman's uniform, particularly his hat, had been redrawn in the French version to make them closer to a French uniform, or at least not so American. This was not the first instance of redrawing a policeman: the American strip of January 18, 1925, appeared the week after in France with the hat and uniform altered. Later that year, the September 27, 1925, French version of the September 13, strip again changed a policeman's hat to make his uniform more French like.

These changes gave Bicot a somewhat unique character. He was at the same time both American and French. Casey Brienza has called this kind of localization of content in comics, domestication.[13] A clear example of this occurred with the July 5, 1925, strip. In the American version Branner had Perry pestering Winnie for fireworks to celebrate July 4th. Passing a construction site Perry helps himself to some sticks of dynamite and paints it red to resemble firecrackers. He tells his friends that he will shoot them off and on hearing this Winnie recruits a policeman to help stop him. They fail and in the second-last panel Perry is shot skyward. In the last panel Winnie wakes from the dream, which had been all the previous panels that day, and agrees to let Perry have fireworks. The strip appeared in *Dimanche Illustré* the following week on July 12. Rather than American Independence Day, Bicot naturally enough wished to celebrate July 14, Bastille Day. Whereas Perry says, "Winnie's a bum patriot! Won't even let me celebrate th' fourth o' July!!" Bicot says "C'est triste, ca!! Elle ne veut même pas me laisser fêter la fête nationale!" [It's sad. She does not even want to let me celebrate National Day]. When Suzy approached the police officer he is again transformed into a more French representation. And Suzy's language is more panicked than Winnie's with her sentence broken up to convey fear and urgency. And when she awakes Suzy, unlike Winnie does not give in to Bicot's demands and instead tells him to "leave me alone with your fireworks." It would seem a bad dream is not enough to cause a French woman to change her mind and give way to a child's wish, or at least the translator found that sentiment inappropriate. The strip then demonstrates a more French sensibility. Even the onomatopoeia "Boom!!" in the 11th panel is translated as "Boum," which literally means bang in English, but would have been less trouble to alter than having to write the French for boom, bôme.

Perry's vocabulary did not always lend itself to an easy translation because it was so idiomatic. For instance, in the strip of June 28, 1925, he arranges a punctured tire for the car of Winnie's friend so that he can get away to play baseball. Having gone for help he tells a garage worker that "a dumb Dora with lot's o' coin got a flat tire down th' street!! Will ya fix it??" "Sure," says the worker, "that's th' way I like 'em – Rich an' dumb!" (Fig. 3.2). In the French version published on July 26, Bicot simply tells the garage owner, "there is a fortune for you if you go to repair a broken down car of two young women down the road." To which the garage owner replies, "I understand I'll go right away!" The translator did not even attempt to replicate the idiom and rendered the playful language of the American strip in a rather flat and direct French. Indeed, most of the Bicot strips lack idiomatic language and graduate school French is enough of a resource for me to understand most of the strips. Google translate managed with translations of slightly more difficult passages because the idioms used are so basic its algorithm captures them. The issue of language raises a number of questions about how French the strip can be if the language is so nonidiomatic. And just as any translation in effect produces a new work, the different way that French as a text works with the images produces in many ways a different comic strip. That is, comic strips, and that art form, in general, rely on a dynamic relationship between image and text to create meaning. A different language, and a shift from idiomatic forms to basic direct forms, suggests that meanings will not only be different, but will be created differently. *Bicot* then is a French comic strip. And yet *Bicot* could not shake certain American veins of humor.

Fig. 3.2 *Winnie Winkle, Chicago Tribune*, June 28, 1925

Stereotyped representations of black people are not limited to Americans. The sociologist Jan Nederveen Pieterse has shown that such images crop up wherever white interests came into contact with black lives.[14] And clearly *Bicot* shows that the French understood such images. Comic art reduces human figures in most instances to types. Although these types developed in range and style along with the expansion of comic strips in America in the early years of the twentieth century, such was not the case for the images of African Americans. The standard representation of African Americans cannot even be graced with the term caricature since almost always into the 1960s (and indeed beyond) such representations were cruel images based on minstrelsy figures. The international appeal of minstrelsy preceded comic strips and in doing so helped American stereotypes and their visualizations become international in form. *Bicot* was both demonstrative of this internationalization and one of the ways that further imprinted such stereotypes on a non-American audience.[15] I neither want to belabor the point of racial representation, nor downplay it, but my point here is more about the interplay between the local and the global. If the translation of Perry into Bicot created a different comic, it was one that still employed the same set of visual tropes. Sometimes these could be repurposed as in the 1924 episode where Sassafras becomes Mamadou, but part of the humor still relied on the preexisting humor encoded in the minstrelsy stereotype. That is even as naming the figure Mamadou might seem to restore some dignity to the character such was not the case because the visual image makes Mamadou yet another name for a minstrelsy figure.

The Perry strip of October 4, 1925, used another minstrelsy figure to create the humorous situation. Winnie volunteers Perry to look after her friend's baby Arthur so that she and her friend can attend a lecture together. Perry is less than impressed because he wanted to spend the time making money for the Rinkeydinks football team. Walking the baby in a baby carriage he notices a help wanted sign in a butcher's window. The butcher needs a boy with a wagon and Perry hits on an idea and asks Liza, a stereotyped representation of an African American girl (a Topsy figure with kinky hair braided into many tails), to take Arthur in her rickety baby carriage. Perry then uses Arthur's carriage to make deliveries. The joke plays out when Winnie and Arthur's mother discover him in Liza's carriage with her little brother. Arthur's mother exclaims "My Baby," which is rendered in a bold larger than usual font. Her words are accompanied by an onomatopoeia "Eeeeeeeee" from her and a "??????" from Winnie. Winnie then goes to find Perry and retrieve the baby carriage. In the American version, there are two other features worth noting. First Branner represented the butcher as having a German accent" "I gotta haf a poy mit a leedle vagon." The translator of the French version did not attempt to replicate this Americanism of linking butchers with German origins. And in the American version Winnie calls her friend Mrs Hall throughout, indicating a measure of respect that seems linked to class difference. This too disappeared in the French version. What remained was the Topsy stereotype.

The Topsy stereotype derived from Harriet Beecher Stowe's novel *Uncle Tom's Cabin*. Stowe's intention was that Topsy would generate sympathy for the plight of children held in slavery. Stowe described Topsy like so: "she was one of the blackest of her race; and her round, shining eyes, glittering as glass beads, moved with quick and restless glances over everything in the room. . . . Her woolly hair was braided in sundry little tails, which stuck out in every direction. The expression of her face was an odd mixture of shrewdness and cunning, over which was oddly drawn, like a veil, an expression of the most doleful gravity and solemnity. She was dressed in a single filthy, ragged garment, made of bagging . . ."[16] Minstrel performers adopted this description to produce the Topsy figure, a picaninny, who was a natural buffoon. Stowe's description adequately covers Branner's Liza. The Topsy figure was so pervasive that the editors of *Judge* magazine, and cartoonist Victor Gillam, looking for a way in 1899 to depict the Philippines national hero Emilio Aguinaldo as a mischievous child thwarting Uncle Sam's good intentions depicted him as Topsy, spelling out his name in the ribbons on the hair braids.

The French version of the baby carriage strip appeared October 11, 1925. The joke plays out much the same way with some slight differences. Liza becomes Julie. Instead of saying "Aw'right Perry" she instead says "Moi bien vouloir Moussie Bicot" [my pleasure to help Mista Bicot]. This somewhat more formal reply, granting Bicot a playful form of mister, seems to have, at the same time, met a French preference for formality, indicated deference and attempted to represent a perceived idiom. In the discovery panel Mrs Hall exclaims, "Oh ciel! Mon enfant!!" (God heavens, my child) and her onomatopoeia shifts to "Ah! Ah! Ah!" Rather than simply saying, as she does in the American version, "this is an outrage" in the French she adds, "I will never forget it." And Winnie does not simply chase after Perry to get the baby carriage back but adds, "Il n'aura pas de treve! " (there will be no truce). *Bicot* then is a French strip, but in form, in its use of American stereotypes, it retains the traces of its American origins. But not always; the

German butcher and the social distinction disappear in this episode. Importantly here what stays is the visual and what disappears is the verbal. Likewise, in a strip published in both America and France on January 27, 1929, Rip Winkle upsets the fruit cart of a vendor. In the American version the vendor shouts after Rip in a stereotypical Italian accent, "You knock'a my fruit stand over I knock'a your block off!!" In the French this simply becomes "Bandit! All my fruits are on the ground." But one look at the strip in French suggested to me that the American version would depict the fruit vendor as an Italian. Again the visual stayed even as the verbal disappeared. In this 1929 strip, Perry's teacher is female, while Bicot's is male, which suggest some predilection for male teachers either in France or on the translator's behalf. An episode as quintessentially American as the November 22, 1925, Perry strip in which he and Winnie engaged in shopping for a Thanksgiving meal was easily converted to a trip to the stores in the French version of November 29. The jokes in the strip required minimal alteration and the only visual reference to Thanksgiving, a turkey sentenced to death by Perry for being unpatriotic for not wanting to die could simply be eliminated because it was in the strip's header panel. A strip of November 18, 1928, had Perry writing a 50-word story as part of a clothing store's competition for a pair of skates. Perry wins the contest by saying his sister bought him a suit at the store and he said "goody" with the goody repeated many times over to make up the word count. In the French version, the contest required only three words as an attestation. After some thought Bicot writes "Vivent Caleçon Frères," roughly Long Live the Caleçon Brothers, the proprietors of the shop. Literally Caleçon Frères translates as the underpants brothers, which was most likely a deliberate piece of slapstick on the translator's part. The puzzle here is, why three words? For an English speaker asked for three words in French one immediate response would be the French national motto: Liberté, égalité, fraternité; words that surely need no translation. Whether or not the translator was attempting to evoke these three words in this comic is unclear and probably unknowable, but what other reason could there be for reducing 50 words to just three and so evoke *La France*? *Bicot* had no single formula for moving American strips into French strips and so any given episode might display more or less of French or American characteristics. And if in one strip things like social distinctions, apparent in the American strip, were left out, or reformulated for a French understanding, then in another the situation might be reversed if French characteristics required say a more formal style of address.

THE OLDER BULLY

On November 9, 1930, Perry encountered a cigarette-smoking tough older kid who had already given the three other Rinkeydinks black eyes. The strip ran the same week in France. This figure, the as-yet-unnamed Butch Baloney (Gaston Panouille in the French, literally an extra, as in a movie extra) menaces Perry/Bicot across several panels before Officer O'Keefe (an unnamed policeman in the French) comes along and escorts Perry/Bicot home, much to Butch/Gaston's frustration. For the next six months or so Branner used Butch/Gaston as the focal point for numerous strips. In these strips, Branner employed storylines and gags somewhat similar to those used by Australian James Bancks from the 1920s onward in his comic strip *Ginger Meggs*. In his strip, Branner used Butch/Gaston to work a number of familiar themes. For instance, Branner could rework his February 4, 1923, strip in which Perry managed to get paid for work Rip had done – shoveling snow. In the Butch/Gaston version published on February 1, 1931, in both America and France he tells Perry/Bicot and Spud/Auguste to "beat it" from their job shoveling snow so that he can make the money. But when Butch goes to collect payment the boys have already done so. The joke plays out the same way in both English and French, the only difference being that the boys momentarily think of finding Officer O'Keefe in the American version and simply a policeman in the French version. The Irish named beat cop may not have been essential in any way to the gag in this strip, but in the comics section of an American newspaper a cop was almost always Irish and not naming him as such would have broken a convention.

The older bully trope had several stock jokes and these played out across American, French, and Australian culture with little variation. Most of these jokes involved a test of wits between those being bullied and the bully. So for instance on November 16, 1930, the week after his debut, the newly named Butch gives chase again to Perry/Bicot, who manages to get home only to be sent out by his mother to have large knives sharpened. Butch catching sight of these beats a strategic retreat. For the bully trope to carry some genuine threat the bully had to triumph on occasion over his prey or otherwise lose any legitimacy. On December 7, 1930, Butch/Gaston managed to trick Perry/Bicot. Having seen him collect some money from Schultz the butcher, Butch/Gaston hatched a plan to obtain the sum. He told Perry/Bicot that he wants to be friends and suggested they play. After several challenges like balancing on a fence and scaling a telegraph pole Butch/Gaston bet Perry/Bicot that he could not manage a handstand. Perry's successful handstand resulted in all the coins dropping from his pocket, much to Butch's delight that his plan worked. Mostly though, Perry/Bicot triumphed over Butch/Gaston. Earlier on November 23, 1930, Perry/Bicot worked for a butcher delivering turkeys in America and chickens in France. Setting out on his first delivery he is ambushed by Butch, who destroys the bird. Butch gets his comeuppance though when Perry/Bicot finally manages to deliver the bird to its destination: Butch's house. Beyond the difference between a turkey for Thanksgiving in the American version and the chicken in the French there are two other differences. First, Butch is as yet unnamed in the French and when ambushed Bicot exclaimed "Diable! L'apache!!," instead of the simpler "Butch" in the American version. And in the American version the butcher is a Mr. Schultz, whereas he is a simple Monsieur in the French. These differences again placed the strip in some liminal space between America and France.

THE STREETS AND PLAY

Just as Skippy and Ginger Meggs experienced problems playing in the street so too did Perry/Bicot and the gang. From July to September 1932 in both the American and French versions Branner had the Rinkeydink/*Rantanplan* club face a crisis of where to play. The boys were forced to relocate the rickety shack that served as their clubhouse when construction started on the vacant lot on which it stood. Perry/Bicot solves the engineering problem of moving the shack by placing four children's wagons under each corner thereby making it mobile. The next week still in search of a new place for the clubhouse Spud/Auguste says in the American version that "they wouldn't let us put our clubhouse on Hogan's lot," a playful reference to the important American comic *Hogan's Alley*. The joke was omitted from the French version. In the American version Perry implores a school janitor to allow the boys to put the shack in the school playground: "What's the good of school playgrounds if we can't play on 'em." His rhetoric fails to move the janitor, the sort of rigid bureaucrat unfortunately so often encountered in supposedly educational institutions. In the French version Bicot tried to persuade an official to let him place the shack in a public garden with of course the same lack of success. This change in the setting of a hoped for locale for the shack, from a playground to a park flowed from a difference between America and France. Progressives in America had sought to direct children's play and in 1906 founded the Playground Association of America.

One of the leaders of that Association, Luther Gulick described the playground as "a device by which a single leader can effectively control the play of a large number of children." For Gulick, the role of the playground movement was to organize play to instill tradition and social norms. Directed play would develop in children the self-control necessary to appreciate the needs of the community as a whole. In Gulick's words, these were "fundamental conditions without which democracy" cannot continue.[17] Children, like Branner's Rinkeydinks, had other ideas about how they should play. A Playground Association study of 1911 revealed that most of the hours children spent in recreation activities were unrelated to the utility of play as perceived by reformers. Children spent a great deal of time watching movies, at vaudeville or burlesque theaters and in pool halls. Likewise, a play census taken on June 23, 1913, in Cleveland revealed that most children were "just fooling" or "doing nothing" during their recreation hours. These two categories included: breaking windows, chalking suggestive words on buildings, throwing mud at street cars, touching girls, looking at pictures of women in tights on billboards, wearing suggestive buttons, stealing, gambling, and drinking. There was nothing particularly perverse about Cleveland's children. Play and sexuality were closely associated in many autobiographies that recalled childhoods of the era, including reformers like Lincoln Steffen's and William Allen White's. The playground movement thought that by organizing children's play into the more formal structure of games they could redirect the energy of play to socially useful purposes.[18] Branner's Rinkeydinks and most of the kids in kid comic strips resisted the socially useful, although their activities were bounded by the norms of good taste as defined by the Chicago *Tribune* and its middle-class readership. The level of explanation offered here as to the meaning and origins of Branner's small joke in one word balloon is evidence of the way that translation of a work between cultures cannot capture the context of a cultural entity. Indeed, in the strips that followed Branner developed something of a critique of organized play, but it appears this would not have been as well understood in France as in America.

The week after on July 17 a smash destroyed the Rinkeydink/ *Rantanplan's* club house after a towrope broke and it careened down hill. The boys rescued the wood, but lacked a place to reconstruct the shack.

The next week Branner has them looking for a place to play. In the American version Pike says, "You'd think they'd leave them gates open after school so kids wouldn't haft'a play on the streets!" In the French Julot says, "Nous serions bien dans cette cour. Mais la grille est fermée!" [We would be in this yard. But the gate is closed!]. In both the American and French versions householders and shop owners, worried about windows getting broken, chase away the boys. After trying to play on other busier streets the boys finally decide to close a street with fake road works signs. The next week, on July 31, when again playing on busy streets, a car knocks down Perry/Bicot and he is taken to hospital. In the American version the car driver who knocks Perry down intends "to give him a good talking too," for playing in the streets. However, on hearing Perry say to the Rinkeydinks that "every town ought'a have a public playground" so children would not have to play in the streets, he reconsiders. In the French version he intends to give Bicot some words of encouragement to get well and Bicot tells the boys to ask him to give us some place to put our shack. On August 7, 1932, in the American version Branner ran a coupon asking for readers to sign up as members of the Rinkeydink Playground Association, although he gave no mailing instructions. The French version also had a coupon, likewise without instructions but requiring monthly dues of one franc. On August 14, the driver of the car, Mr Dowry in the American version, arranges a club for the boys, complete with gym, running track swimming pool, and baseball field. But their attempts to use all these are constrained by rules requiring them to wear clothes to swim and not to slide into bases. In the French version the baseball field becomes a football (soccer) field and the worry is that if they use it their ball will break a window. After moving their shack to the site on August 21 the boys were evicted on August 28 because Mr Dowry's mortgage had been foreclosed in the American version. In the French an officious new guardian of the villa shoos them out. In this sequence of strips Branner displayed some of his ambiguities with the direction of modern American society. The clearest expression of this attitude occurred in the daily *Winnie Winkle* strips that Branner so often used to criticize consumer desire and artifice over substance. Indeed to read the Sunday strips without this context removes some of the edge to Branner's humor. In the case of these strips, it is clear enough in the American versions that Branner is not only critical of the lack of public play spaces for children, but also worried about the curtailment of their free play. The French versions carry less of that sentiment.

PHYSICAL DIFFERENCE

One significant difference between Perry and *Bicot* was that the *Chicago Tribune* was a broadsheet and *Dimanche Illustré* a tabloid. From a side-by-side comparison of the two versions of the strip it seems that the French publisher simply reproduced the full-page broadsheet comic strip at a reduced tabloid size. But from January 1933 the *Chicago Tribune* reduced the Sunday *Winnie Winkle* strip that featured Perry to a half page. *Dimanche Illustré* continued to publish *Bicot* as a full separate page until October 10, 1937, when the strip, still at full-page height, became the central element of a triptych of three comics, spread over two pages. This required a different process for reproduction and individual panels were cropped to fit the French tabloid. On October 2, 1938, *Dimanche Illustré* ceased its spread of comics and *Bicot* was reduced to a single row of five to six panels for several weeks before being relaunched on November 13, 1938, as *Bicot et Suzy* with two rows of up to 12 panels occupying less than a quarter of a page. *Bicot et Suzy* retained this format until what seems to have been its last appearance on May 26, 1940.

The translation of Perry Winkle comics into French as *Bicot* created a French kid comic, but one that carried distinctly American characteristics. Both in form, such as word balloons, and in content, such as baseball games, *Bicot* signaled its American origins. Nonetheless, the effort at giving the strip a French character such as removing overt Americanisms and on occasions giving Bicot and his friends a more French sensibility produced a comic that resonated enough with French readers to warrant annual collections between 1926 and 1939 and the reprinting of those collections in the 1960s. *Bicot* then might be thought of then as an early form of glocalization or domestication of a comic.[19]

NOTES

1. Paul Jacques Dupuy (1878–1927), Assemblée nationale, http://www.assemblee-nationale.fr/sycomore/fiche.asp?num_dept=2741#biographie.
2. La Cité internationale de la bande dessinée et de l'image, "L'Excelsior Dimanche – Le Dimanche," Illustré"http://collections.citebd.org/in/faces/details.xhtml?id=46d2e8f5-889f-4b1e-a3b0-2f213a3e4e6f.
3. The boys are named in the June 29, 1924, episode in *Excelsior Dimanche*.
4. *French poems, nursery rhymes and riddles*, https://en.wikisource.org/wiki/French_poems,_nursery_rhymes_and_riddles.

5. John Kuo Wei Tchen, *New York Before Chinatown: Orientalism and the Shaping of American Culture, 1776–1882* (Baltimore: Johns Hopkins University Press, 1999); Herbert Asbury, *Gangs of New York: An Informal History Of The Underworld* (New York: Thunder's Mouth Press, 2001 [1927]); Mary Ting Yi Lui, *The Chinatown Trunk Mystery: Murder, Miscegenation, and Other Dangerous Encounters in Turn-of-the-Century New York City* (Princeton: Princeton University Press, 2005). *Historical Census Statistics on the Foreign-Born Population of the United States: 1850–2000*, https://www.census.gov/population/www/documentation/twps0081/tables/tab14.xls

6. Michelle Guillon, "The Chinese and Chinese Districts in Paris," in *The Last Half Century of Chinese Overseas*, Elizabeth Sinn, editor (Hong Kong: Hong Kong University Press, 1998), 185–200.

7. Joe Lunn, "'Les Races Guerrieres': Racial Preconceptions in the French Military about West African Soldiers during the First World War," *Journal of Contemporary History*, Vol. 34, No. 4 (1999): 517–536.

8. Wen Shuang, "Mediated Imaginations: Chinese-Arab Connections in the Late Nineteenth and Early Twentieth Centuries," Georgetown University, PhD 2015.

9. Henri Mendras with Alistair Cole, *Social Change in Modern France: Towards a Cultural Anthropology of the Fifth Republic* (New York: Cambridge University Press, 1991), 32.

10. Martha H. Patterson, ed. *The American New Woman Revisited* (New Brunswick: Rutgers University Press, 2008).

11. Richard Weiss, *The American Myth of Success: From Horatio Alger to Norman Vincent Peale* (New York: Basic Books, 1969).

12. Josh Chetwynd, *Baseball in Europe: A Country by Country History* (Jefferson, NC: McFarland, 2008), 157–172.

13. Casey Brienza, *Manga in America: Transnational Book Publishing and the Domestication of Japanese Comics* (London: Bloomsbury Academic, 2016)

14. Jan Nederveen Pieterse, *White on Black: Images of Africa and Blacks in Western Popular Culture* (New Haven: Yale University Press, 1992).

15. David Pettersen, "Transnational Blackface, Neo-Minstrelsy and the 'French Eddie Murphy' in Intouchables," *Modern & Contemporary France*, Vol. 24, No. 1 (2016): 51–69, doi:10.1080/09639489.2015.1092430; Stephen Johnson, "Introduction: The Persistence of Blackface and the Minstrel Tradition," in *Burnt Cork: Traditions and Legacies of Blackface Minstrelsy*, Stephen Johnson, editor (Boston: University of Massachusetts Press, 2012), 1–17.

16. Harriet Beecher Stowe, *Uncle Tom's Cabin* (New York: Library of America, 1982), 278.

17. Luther H. Gulick, *A Philosophy of Play* (New York: C. Scribner's Sons, 1920), 12, 236, 242, 265.
18. Dominick J. Cavallo, *Muscles and Morals: Organized Playgrounds and Urban Reform, 1880–1920* (Philadelphia: University of Pennsylvania Press, 1981); Rowland Haynes, "Recreation Survey, Milwaukee, Wisconsin," *Playground*, Vol. 6 (May 1912): 38–73; Bernard Mergen, *Play and Playthings: A Reference Guide* (Westport, CT: Greenwood, 1982), 33, 70–71.
19. Roland Robertson, Gocalization: Time-space and Homogeneity-heterogeneity," in *Global Modernities*, Mike Featherstone, Scott Lash, and Roland Robertson, editors (London: Sage Publications, 1995), 25–44.

CHAPTER 4

America and Britain: Dennis the Menace (s)

Abstract This chapter compares the British and American *Dennis the Menace* comic strips arguing that despite so many similarities and a common genre the different history of the form in those countries led to two very different comics. These two comics are more distinct from each other than, for instance, *Skippy* and *Ginger Meggs*. Yet, in both comics, race is mostly absent from the content, and yet present by its very absence.

Keywords Hank Ketcham · David Law · *Beano* · Sambo · Stereotypes · Class

Comparing the British and American *Dennis the Menace* comics seems given in a book arguing for a comparative approach to international histories of comics through genre. Not only did the two features start in the same year and the same month, but also more or less in the same week and most likely appeared on the same day. The American version appeared on March 12, 1951. The British comic first appeared in the *Beano* #452 (March 17, 1951). One version of this history has it that in the 1950s British comic magazines that were dated Saturday went on sale the previous Monday and so it seems likely the two appeared on the same day.[1] But, there the similarities end in so many ways.

The American *Dennis the Menace* appeared as a single-panel feature in daily newspapers and after 1952 as a Sunday comic strip. Hank Ketcham,

© The Author(s) 2016
I. Gordon, *Kid Comic Strips*, Palgrave Studies in Comics and Graphic Novels, DOI 10.1057/978-1-137-55580-9_4

who created the strip, had worked as an animator for Walter Lanz and Disney before working on various projects to promote War Bonds during World War II. During the war, he began freelancing cartoons to publications such as *The Saturday Evening Post*. After the war, he set up shop as a freelancer in Westport, Connecticut, before moving to California in 1948. The story goes that in October 1950 while he was at work on a cartoon for *The Saturday Evening Post* his wife Alice entered the studio to exclaim, "your son is a menace." Recognizing a crucial element of a successful comic, a distinctive character, Ketcham used his son's name to arrive at *Dennis the Menace* and sold it as a feature to the Post-Hall Syndicate. The comic grew from its original 16 newspapers to 100 within a year and by 1959 a live-action television series appeared. The usual array of tie-in merchandise followed, as did several series of comic books. By the time Ketcham died in 2001 the comic appeared in over 1,000 newspapers in 48 countries.

The British *Dennis* appeared weekly in the children's comics magazine *Beano*. There is no immediate American equivalent of *Beano* and its stable mate *Dandy*. Indeed, *Beano* may best be known in America for the *John Myall and the Blues Breakers with Eric Clapton* album cover for which Clapton was photographed reading the May 7, 1966, issue. The magazines though were distributed widely in other English-speaking domains and children in former British colonies such as Australia, Canada, and Singapore read them with some regularity. According to an article in the *Daily Mail*, the *Beano* editorial team conceived of the British *Dennis the Menace* in 1950. George Moonie, Ian Chisholm, and David Law were working on creating a mischievous character that would build on Law's kid strip work for the *Evening Telegraph*, but make the character brasher. Law was sketching concepts, but none seemed to jell and a frustrated Chisholm roughed out an image on a Player's Cigarette pack.[2] The origins then of the two comics, or at least the origin stories, are different. The American version was the product of individual talent. The British work a communal, or committee, effort. Nonetheless, even as the American *Dennis* continued to be published over Ketcham's signature he hired a series of assistants including an art assistant, Lee Holley, and a gag writer, Bob Harmon. There is a certain irony in that the comic created by a group was then produced by an individual for years and that the comic created by an individual swiftly became a small enterprise. Law did not sign his work. And so we have the *Beano's Dennis the Menace* and Hank Ketcham's *Dennis the Menace*.[3]

The comics were created under very different conditions. Ketcham in Carmel, California, would have already been experiencing the effects of the large postwar economic book in America and the suburbanization and embourgeoisement of the society producing both a new group of white collar workers and lessening income disparity between blue and white collar workers.[4] In Britain, petrol rationing after World War II had only ended in mid-1950. Sugar remained rationed until September 1953. In 1951 the meat ration was reduced for a time and meat was not de-rationed until June 1954. The historian Ina Zweiniger-Bargielowska suggests that such rationing was part of the cause of a deeply divided society in Britain in the late 1940s and early 1950s.[5] In some ways, the first episode of both comics captures some of the mood of their respective countries. The British Dennis cannot resist walking on the grass in a park clearly labeled with a sign to keep off. His father then removed the leash from his dog (another sign says dogs must be leashed) and places it on his son. It is very tempting to read a longing to be out from under the strictures of a society into this strip. To do so would require making an argument for some special poignancy in this version of a joke as old as city bureaucracies posting signs forbidding walking on the grass. *Beano* announced the strip with a heading that read, "Look! Here's a new pal you'll enjoy – He's the world's wildest boy!" Under this a head shot of a growling Dennis precedes the strip title that is followed by three more head shots: a man who has taken a pie to the face, a shocked woman, and a policeman with an arrow through his helmet. So, if the joke was already tired in 1951, at least the strip promised some slapstick wildness.

Much to his parents' chagrin in the first American comic Dennis says to a traffic cop, who has pulled his father over, "You didn't catch us! We ran out of gas!" The cop looks nonplussed and not in a pleasant fashion. This Dennis then is a wiseacre and the comic seems to promise a child who exposes the foibles of the adult world. For instance, in the episode of March 17, 1951, standing behind the couch overhearing his father talk to a friend Dennis says, "Hey Mom! Bring the soap and wash out Daddy's mouth!" But in the early years at least the American Dennis was just as capable of direct mischief as his British namesake. On March 16, 1951, the comic had a cop talking on a beat phone with Dennis handcuffed to him. The conversation goes, "and I says, 'Get off the grass' and he says, 'make me' and I says...." As old as it was the joke still worked on both sides of the Atlantic. But the American *Dennis* showed a more prosperous society, his father drives a car, the family lives in a white picket fence clearly middle-class (and white) neighborhood. Compared with the British comic, the American *Dennis* projects a self-assured middle-class sensibility.

But the certainty of the American Dennis's family's social standing *vis-à-vis* the British Dennis's position does not imply that the British character's family was working class.

In the first year, Ketcham pitched the American comic at an adult audience. To be sure the funny pages in American newspapers in the 1950s attracted a wide audience both young and old. In 1950, among adult men and women who read newspapers the median range of comic strip readership was at least 75 % across the USA.[6] The American *Dennis* was not averse to noticing adult sexuality. So, for instance, on February 27, 1951, he introduced a friend Billy to his mother and added, "Some looker, eh?" On May 25, 1951, Ketcham had Dennis and his father waiting at a train station. When Dennis's father Henry stared after at an attractive woman who walked pass Dennis says, "But Daddy, anybody can see that isn't Grandma!" On July 24 that year Dennis told a sailor seated on a park bench near his mother to beat it because "she's married to my Dad." Beach outings too were opportunities for jokes about adult foibles. On July 28, Dennis and his father manage to get the name and phone number of a pretty girl while getting ice creams and Alice, his mother, is less than impressed on hearing this news from Dennis. On August 20 in a rare two-panel comic, Dennis asks his Dad to "take a look at the cute little blonde" who to Henry's displeasure on turning over from sun tanning turns out to be a child. On September 9, 1951, when Dennis interrupts his mother in the bath to introduce Joey and ask him, "Isn't she pretty?" The comic is not quite chessecake, but walks a line between youthful innocence and adult knowingness, and does so in this case with a wink. On December 6, 1951, Alice entertains an attractive woman guest, to which Dennis says, "Wow! Has Daddy seen her?" And on December 21 that year Dennis comments of a store Santa that "he's loaded! And not with presents" with the illustration showing an inebriated Santa depicted with the little circles swimming about Santa's head that comics use to indicate such a state. And so it went: on December 12, 1951, Dennis and his father had clearly been to a cabaret and not the zoo; on March 7, 1952, Dennis announces that Henry is home when he is clearly trying to creep in late. These sorts of gags continued through much of the life of the comic. For instance, on February 6, 1961, Dennis says to a good-looking woman visiting his mother, "Dad is sure gonna be surprised to see you! He told Mom he didn't know you were alive!" Sometimes though, Ketcham toned the comic down a little in this regard. In four episodes from March 23 to August 8, 1951, he had Henry and Alice sleeping in a double bed.

By October 3 they were in twin beds. In 1952 they were in a double bed
January 1, and November 6, but in twin beds April 9 and May 29. Mostly
after that they were in a double bed. Whether the type of bed represented
some effort at censorship or simply artistic choice is unclear. In this same
period on television, even real-life couples such as Lucille Ball and Desi
Arnaz had to be shown sleeping in twin beds, so newspapers might have
been uncomfortable with Henry and Alice in the same bed. As a gag
cartoonist Ketcham was no doubt used to creating humor for more
adult magazine readers. His *Dennis* certainly always had a more diverse
and an adult audience unlike the *Beano's Dennis*.

KETCHAM'S DENNIS AN ADULT STRIP?

Several features clearly distinguished Ketcham's *Dennis* from the British
Dennis. First, the American *Dennis* as a daily panel was mostly a gag strip
and appeared more regularly than the British comic. Just as with the
difference between *Ginger Meggs* and the daily *Skippy* the different frequency created different forms and means to fill the comic. One of
Dennis's stock in trade was a tendency to be overly frank at the wrong
moment. Ketcham used at least 34 of these gags between 1951 and 1954.
These ranged in style from the April 25, 1951, episode in which Dennis
shouted to his mother that an "old windbag" was on the phone and
asking, "shall I tell her you're out again?" to Dennis telling his father in
a diner on September 2, 1954, that, "My spoon isn't greasy!" Ketcham, or
his gag writers, settled in to this sort of gag as a feature of the comic in late
1951. On October 29 Dennis tells a caller his father is not home because
of a fight with his mother. The next day he tells a woman that her baby
looks a lot like his grandpa. Dennis then moves to embarrassing his
mother when she has visitors by asking her on November 16, 1951,
which of the three women playing cards with her "gets sore when she
doesn't win." At a dinner party on February 2, 1952, he embarrassed his
mother again by observing that the roast "looks swell" and no one would
know she had "dropped it." Dennis revealed that there were "ants in the
bread bin" to a group of women enjoying sandwiches on May 16 and that
his father had criticized the butcher on June 3. On June 27 Ketcham
switched the perspective from the present to the aftermath when Henry
says to a departing guest, "Listen Frank! Alice is delighted to have you for
dinner regardless of what Dennis says!" And to a guest on September 9,
1952, Dennis said, "Gee your hat is big! No wonder Dad said you were a

fathead." This latter gag contained an element of word play and Ketcham developed this style of gag further. So on July 5, 1953, a guest arrives and Dennis says, "He came in a car Dad! I thought you said he was on a wagon!" with Dennis not understanding "on the wagon" meant not drinking alcohol. On July 22 the gag was about Mr. Wilson's spare tire clearly revealed as meaning his girth. On November 9, 1953, he asked a man visiting the Mitchell family with his wife where the hen pecked him. On November 23 the plumber did not look like a "highway robber." And when visiting an eccentric looking man with his parents on April 23, 1954, Dennis asks him, "Where do you keep your Belfry Mr Wedge? I'd like to see your bats."

The American Dennis's playful use of words also occurred in situations other than embarrassing moments for his parents. For instance, on November 26, 1954, he said to his father, "Why get sore 'cause your pipe won't draw? You don't see me tryin' to smoke crayons, do ya?" David Law in the *Beano* also tried his hand at word play jokes. On October 23, 1954, Dennis's father tells him to always share sweets. Dennis arranges for boys to take away the furniture from his house and his father on waking up gets it back and scolds Dennis for deliberately misunderstanding him to mean sharing suites of furniture. On November 27 in *Beano* a press photographer after a scoop pestered Dennis about his misdeeds. Eventually, Dennis has him buried under a pile of sand and standing over the photographer says, "Here's a scoop! Scoop your way out!" while handing him a small hand-scoop. Law's jokes were more one-dimensional than Ketcham's offering only the humor of the word play and not the parental embarrassment that so often went with the American Dennis's comments. The *Beano* comics also seem more forced in their humor offering didactic moments of language instruction to ten-year-olds rather than the innocence of childhood humor of the American strip.

Eric Clapton, who apparently still read the *Beano* at age 21, notwithstanding the magazine was aimed more at children with the prime reading age probably being somewhere between 10 and 12. Indeed, *Beano's* publishers D. C. Thomson stated on their website in 2016 that it is "aimed primarily at boys aged seven-11 (although nearly a third of our readers comprise the coolest girls in this age group)."[7] The true heyday of the *Beano* was in April 1950 when it sold 1,974,072 copies per issue. By 2015 that figure had shrunk to around 37,000 copies.[8] The perceived audience of young boys though has remained a constant. The 1951 issues of the *Beano* are not available at the British Library, but a review of the

1952 episodes of the British Dennis reveals not a single instance of a joke with an adult theme, not so much as a subtle double entendre for an older audience. The *Beano* then offered different comic fare than American comic strip pages in newspapers. The *Beano's* audience was children and the American comic strip's a polysemic mixture of adults and children. The two Menaces though did share some gag similarities, beyond the walking on the grass joke, with both working old standards and variations on other themes.

WINDOWS, CRASHES, AND SWANS

Despite their different audiences the two Menaces shared some similar situations. These played out differently though, in part because the British Dennis was for children, and in part because the American Dennis was mostly a single-panel comic. So, for instance, David Law could have his Dennis in the *Beano* engage in a similar sort of downhill out-of-control mayhem as Ginger and Skippy, albeit on a bicycle. A strip of January 19, 1952, had Dennis and three others riding a single bike. After the inevitable crash, Dennis's father reduces it to a monocycle to prevent future mishaps. On February 27, 1954, Dennis's father is in a wheelchair and Law occupied some of the strip with a bit of downhill mayhem before setting up another joke of Dennis losing his Dad after abandoning him outside a cinema. In a strip of August 20, 1955, the gag revolves around the various uses Dennis has for chairs. His father insists chairs are for sitting on. At one point Dennis uses a chair with casters to careen downhill, where he runs into Dad, as he always inevitably does. Chairs are then put to another use as something to bend over to receive a beating with the slipper. These types of comics require at least a few panels and lay beyond the scope of the daily American *Dennis*. To be sure, an artist can depict movement and even something of a narrative in a single panel through various methods like little cloud puffs at the feet of a character drawn in the foreground or mid-foreground of a panel and angled slightly forward, which indicates running, such as in the December 24, 1952, episode of Ketcham's strip. Another method is to show multiple renderings of a limb to indicate movement, which Ketcham used on December 3, 1952, to show Henry searching for his glasses that Dennis has grabbed in an attempt to prevent a spanking. And yet another method is to structure a single panel so that it can contain a narrative, such as the December 12, 1952, episode in which Dennis rides the down escalator, much to the displeasure of his mother on the up escalator, who had told him to wait at the top. But the sort of narrative that the downhill mayhem gag required was mostly beyond the scope of Ketcham's comic. The American *Dennis* had three basic frames of action that the one panel might represent: Prelude, Event, and Aftermath. So a reader might imagine the mayhem to ensure when Dennis and four other children pile on top of Henry on January 6, 1953, as he prepares to take off on a snow toboggan, but the gag is mostly from Henry's discomfort. On December 9, 1961, Ketcham had Dennis moving swiftly on his tricycle with his young playmate Margaret standing on the rear platform and holding on for dear life. She says, "For Heaven's sake, slow down! And stop your zigzagging! And watch out for the . . . " This comic's gag is in what is about to happen and nicely works the prelude frame of action. On February 5, 1962, Ketcham managed to work both an Aftermath and a Prelude mise-en-scène into a single panel. In the fore-ground Dennis and Henry are on a sled. Dennis holds the steering reigns and turns to his father to say, "I thought you were steering!" Henry holds on to his hat and has a worried look. The background shows that that the two have zipped down a mountain slope at speed zigzagging through a range of trees. These frames of action though better allowed for variations on the broken window gag, although Ketcham often had to stretch to two panels to pull off these jokes.

A Ketcham panel from April 19, 1951, shows Dennis and two playmates standing in a living room amid the rubble of a broken window, vase, and a lamp. As the two look on thoughtfully Dennis offers, "That takes care of the window and vase. Now, how did we break the lamp?" On October 22, 1951, in another of his occasional two-panel Dennis's Ketcham has Henry say to Alice and Dennis, "we'll, if he broke a window, we'll just have to pay . . . " And in the second panel in a masterful double take rendered with movement lines and a faint before and fuller now rendition of Henry's face " . . . in a Department Store?!!!" At the same time Dennis runs from the room with the little cloud-bursts of speed rendered behind his departing figure. On April 14, 1953, Ketcham again used two panels to have Henry do a double take on realizing Dennis has hit a ball through a home's window and not as he first thought a home run. On May 6, 1954, Dennis told his father he had hit a home run and Henry is dutifully proud until he learns that, "it'll only cost six dollars for the window." And in yet another two-panel comic on May 19, 1961, Dennis says, "Mr. Wilson won't let us have our ball!" The next panel shows Henry looking at Mr. Wilson through a broken panel of glass (a small triumph of craft) and the latter's line is, "Looking for something." Most of the time Ketcham could even manage a broken window gag without the presence of a window. A comic from October 11, 1953, shows Dennis standing in the foreground with a model fighter plane that has a wind up propeller. In the background, another boy points to Dennis and the caption reads: "He's our ace. Five windows broken and four probables." Another from January 22, 1954, has Dennis rushing in to pose a question to his father, "Do you know that big picture window the Wilson's used to have?" Is this latter comic, Ketcham had so well established Dennis's character and mastered the use of a single panel that the implication for the reader and Henry is clear: Dennis has broken the window.

Law also worked the broken window/glass theme with one of his first efforts on August 9, 1952, a strip that played on the Emperor has no Clothes tale. Dennis and his friends pretend to be holding a piece of plate glass and various adults give them a wide berth. Eventually a small boy riding a scooter, and knowing no better, destroys their conceit by riding through the middle of the imagined plate glass. In a *Beano* strip of January 2, 1954, Dennis unleashed a mighty kick and his football sailed over a garden wall and a loud crash of breaking glass emitted. Perturbed that his balls never come back Dennis decides to construct a boomerang because it will always return. In a spate of action that follows he manages to break another window before his Dad catches up with him and uses the boomerang to wallop him. Dennis bent over for his punishment notes, "it always comes back to me." In an inventive strip of January 23, 1954, Law had Dennis meet another of *Beano's* characters *Minnie the Minx*. Dennis swapped his slingshot with Minnie for her doll pram. He used her pram to deliberately bump into people and to generally get up to no good, including using it to take a fast ride down a hill. He also manages to get into a fight, much to his pleasure, with bullies who take him for a "cissy." After swapping back with Minnie he discovers she used his slingshot to break many windows. Dennis's father handing out the usual punishment, a beating with a slipper, tells Dennis "no lies" when he insists he was playing with a doll's pram. As part of a larger situation about Dennis learning to appreciate his grandmother, Law had Grannie kick a football through a window on April 30, 1955, and then trip up a policeman, who was naturally enough chasing Dennis. Law found an even better breaking glass gag using the preexisting menace reputation of Dennis on September 10, 1955. After Dad burns all of Dennis's slingshots (catapults in the strip) to prevent any more broken glass payments, he forces Dennis to take a quiet walk with him. A plane breaking the sound barrier and causing all the glass in a hothouse to break interrupts

Fig. 4.1   *Dennis the Menace, The Beano,* September 10, 1955

their walk. Both Dad and Dennis run for it because such damage is sure to be blamed on Dennis (Fig. 4.1).

The point here is that despite the very different audiences the artists and publishers aimed the Menaces at the two comics managed to find common themes. Across all six strips and all four countries examined here then there was humor to be found in broken windows even within the narrative limits of a panel comic. While much of the humor in the American *Dennis* had a whimsical nature, the sort of whimsy that flows from economic certainty that bordered on complacency, sometimes the strip drifted into the slapstick cruelty of the British strip. On June 14, 1951, one swan swimming on a lake warns another to stay away from the kid in black pants, the American Dennis. The reason to avoid him is not stated directly, but represented by the knot in the swan's neck. This of course is a flight of the imagination, and unlike many of the gags in the American *Dennis*, impossible. This episode then had more in common with the British *Dennis's* style of humor. On July 19, 1952, Dennis attached an outboard motor to the back of a swan that had been overcurious and aggressive about his model sailboat on a pond. In general though, the British Dennis operated in the realm of wild impossible slapstick, whereas the American Dennis worked a vein of situation comedy.

The Menace, Dennis, and the Barber's Shop

The characters in the *Beano's Dennis* often referred to the title character simply as the Menace. On February 20, 1954, wrestlers and the crowd at a match shun "the Menace." So well known as a menace was this Dennis that in an episode of March 6, 1954, when he visited the circus, lions knowing who he was refused to let him stick his head in their mouths in replication of a circus performer's trick. Likewise, a bucking horse became passive with Dennis on its back. Even the police found Dennis intimidating with numerous Bobbies shunning duty in their district in a strip of June 19, 1954. Visiting the zoo on February 19, 1955, a character refers to him as the "famous menace." Over and over again in the *Beano*, people saw Dennis and knew trouble would follow. Because the American comic was mostly just a panel this sense of anticipated trouble by Dennis's mere presence seldom existed in that feature. Occasionally though, Ketcham managed to work the preexisting reputation theme into his comic; for instance, on May 31, 1954, Alice tells Dennis not to scare the tiger in a cage at the zoo. On April 28, 1953, Henry places Dennis on a horse's back. The horse turns to look at Dennis and he asks, "Dad! What's he lookin' at me for?" A wrangler in the background compliments the horse's look and Dennis's question by being positioned in a pose that suggests some concern. The American Dennis's reputation was the focus again on August 26, 1953, when a tree teeters over a house on the street about to tumble and destroy it Alice says to a tearful Dennis, "No one said you did it. Don't be so self-conscious." On February 4, 1954, all Ketcham needed was a caption, "I don't think he did it Henry. The lights are out all over the neighborhood" to illustrate a black blob. The American Dennis's reputation preceded him to the barber's shop, but this was more due to encounters with him than a generalized spread of his fame as a menace. Even on his first visit to the barber's on April 5, 1951, the gag read, "Be fair about it Bert...I cut his hair last time!" On June 19, 1952, a barber glances out his window at Dennis and his mother and says, "Thank goodness! They're going right on past!" And on October 16, 1954, one barber tells another to hurry up with the No Children sign because "his mother is looking this way."

The British Dennis had a constant target for his bullying in Walter a bespectacled classmate who often, by my count at least 30 times between 1952 and 1962, bore the brunt of Dennis's pranks. Walter has since become known as Walter the softie, but in these years he was simply Walter. Indeed as late as June 5, 1965, Dennis's most accusatory adjective for Walter was "swot," that is someone of superior academic skills. Dennis himself through circumstance was labeled a "cissy" in three early strips, on January 23, 1954; February 19, 1955; and April 30, 1955. In each instance he turned the situation to his advantage. Finally, on May 22, 1965, the British Dennis suggested Walter was a cissy for liking a Bo-Peep nursery rhyme and Law drew Walter dressed as Bo-Peep with the word "simper" as a descriptor above his head, which made Walter campy in the manner of British actor Kenneth Williams then a featured player in the *Carry On* series of films. The American *Dennis* also engaged at least once in labeling playmates in a derogatory fashion. On January 25, 1959, he asked his playmate Joey "ya wanna grow up to be a sissy?" to which Joey lisped in reply "Yeth!" But on the whole the preexisting reputation as "the menace," and a style of humor that incorporated acts of bullying, belonged more to the British *Dennis*.

The different ways in which Ketcham and Law used the barber shop as a site of gags also reveals something about the two comics's very different basis of humor. Law set the action of the British *Dennis* in a barber's only twice in the years up to 1962. On May 24, 1952, after being thwarted from scalping his usual target for bullying, the as yet unnamed Walter, while playing Cowboys and Indians Dennis and a friend take charge of a barber's shop when the owner takes his lunch break. The friend stands on Dennis's shoulders and they put a coat on covering their frames, and in the world of the British *Dennis* no one twigs to this subterfuge, and the two as one appear to be the barber. A customer arrives and Dennis's friend shaves his head bald. Peeking out from under the coat Dennis realizes the customer is his father who complains of having been scalped. On April 7, 1962, Dennis is again playing Cowboys and Indians and dashes into a hairdressing salon, actually a barber's but run by a man named Pierre with a cartoon version of a French accent. Mayhem ensures with a customer catapulted into the ceiling from an ascending chair. Later, while still playing the same game Dennis, to avoid being "scalped," runs into a freshly laid cement path. Stuck in the setting cement, Pierre, whose path it of course is, takes his revenge by shaving Dennis's head. Dennis walks away muttering "scalped after all!" David Law's only use of a barber's shop for the locales of Dennis strips was associated with Cowboy and Indian games and the joke revolved around scalping. This British strip then was in part domesticating the notion of children playing cowboys, something derived from American media.

Ketcham used the barbers for a more complex range of jokes beyond Dennis's reputation preceding him, but did not try a scalping joke. Ketcham did use Cowboy themes, but not that I have seen Cowboy and Indian themes. In the May 17, 1951, panel as Dennis fidgets in the chair his barber says to another, "If this was an electric chair, I'd be tempted to turn on the juice." This comic might seem like a particularly grim joke, but the smile of recognition on the second barber's face situates the gag as exasperated rhetoric of the sort that a parent might use with a difficult child, and not a literal intention. Ketcham showed a lighter touch on July 27, 1951, with Dennis sitting on a bench placed across the arms of the barber's chair turning to an adult customer positioned below Dennis in his chair and reading a magazine. The line is, "Lemme see that when you're through with it, will you, Shorty?" The humor here lays in the incongruity of a child speaking to an adult in such a fashion. A month later on August 27 a barber sits in a chair amidst a scene of destruction in his shop. He says to the concerned-looking cop at his door, "Little kid 'bout five... didn't want his hair cut... mother insisted." Even though Ketcham drew a scene of ruin, with some exaggeration of the damage an out-of-control child might wrought, he stayed within the boundaries of the possible. Law's Dennis in the *Beano* knew no such bounds. Ketcham balanced his Dennis causing mayhem barber gags with more subdued gags. So the August 27, 1951, destruction gag sits between the July 27 incongruity gag, and a December 11, 1951 aftermath gag in which Dennis says to his mother as they leave the shop, "He must be learning to count. He kept counting up to ten all the time I was in the chair." Earl the barber glares from the shop at the departing Dennis. The barber's shop as a male domain was as Gerard Jones reminds us in *Men of Tomorrow* a place where men might if they wished obtain under the counter publications and the like.[9] Ketcham managed to reference this aspect in a strip of July 5, 1961, in which Dennis tells his mother returning to collect him and pay for his hair cut that, "You shoulda been here an' heard all the jokes! Ya know what Pat said to Mike when the cow…" The two barbers look ashen faced and one noticeably sweats at this revelation of blue jokes told in the presence of Dennis.

ABSENCE OF RACE?

The absence of more barbershop humor from the British *Dennis* seems somewhat odd. As noted, the early American *Dennis* featured beat cops, but these soon disappeared from the strip going the way of the Irish cop as the subject for jokes. The notion of a cop walking a beat in the suburbs was a stretch and the jokes subsided. More importantly though is the almost complete absence of race jokes in both comics. The years between 1951 and 1962 fall into somewhat of an interregnum in which the old racist stereotyped images began to disappear from newspaper comics and before a perceived need to have racial diversity in comics produced a new wave of less stereotypical figures. In Ketcham's case, he only used an African American character twice and both instances occurred in 1970 outside the period of this study. Nonetheless, Ketcham's attempts at representing race say something about his *Dennis the Menace*. In both instances his intent in the joke was to have Dennis appear innocent of race while at the same time making that day's episode wholly about race.

On May 13, 1970, Ketcham used an African American character named Jackson who apparently was a neighbor of Dennis's. Visually, Jackson was a Sambo stereotype and Ketcham remained tone deaf to how deeply offensive such a representation was, and always had been. Certainly, by 1970 many editors found such a representation unacceptable, although others did not. The caption of that day's comic read "I'm havin' some race trouble with Jackson. He runs faster than I do." Not all newspapers that carried the comic ran it that day, but the episode did run across the country in papers including the *Independent* from Long Beach, California; the Fayetteville *Northwest Arkansas Times;* and early editions of the *Washington Post.* As Ketcham tells the story protests "started in Detroit, then moved south to St. Louis where rocks and bottles were thrown through the windows of the *Post-Dispatch*." In his autobiography Ketcham goes on to say,

> I made a point not to apologize but to express my utter dismay at the absurd reaction to my innocent cartoon and my amazement at the number of 'art directors' out there. Any regular Dennis-watcher would surely know that I

am never vindictive or show any intent to malign or denigrate. But I guess those violent protestants [sic] were not avid followers of newspaper comics. And they weren't complaining about the "gag"; it was my depiction of Dennis's new pal that got their tails in a knot. I gave them a miniature Stepin Fetchit when they wanted a half-pint Harry Belafonte.

In this volume Ketcham also includes what he says "was a milder version of Dennis' black neighbor, Jackson. Earlier in a fit of lapsus noodle I concocted a lampoon that caused chaos and anguish."[10] Perhaps Ketcham suffered from a terrible memory, a lack of research skills even in his own files, or was, at best, dissembling. The milder version that he suggests came later had appeared on January 6, 1970, four months earlier than the racist stereotype version. The milder version depicts Jackson in a less stereotypical manner. The gag is that Dennis thinks they're exactly the same except Jackson is left-handed. It is not a great joke, but it is not as offensive visually. Ketcham does remember correctly in that he did not apologize. His letter to newspaper editors explaining the May 13, 1970, episode appeared in several papers. His language was somewhat similar to that in his autobiography expressing his "great dismay" on learning of the "adverse reaction" to the May 13 episode. He pleads that, "Surely, if I had dreamed it possible that anyone would have been offended, I would have never drawn the cartoon." This seems a strange way of putting the issue because it suggests that he would draw racial stereotypes if people were not offended, and indeed that was the case. Ketcham went on to say, "I don't wish to give you the impression that drawing Jackson in this style was a hasty decision." He then says that after Jackson's initial appearance on January 6 the response was so favorable that he decided "to work up a new design concept . . . more in keeping with the caricatures of Dennis and his playmates." Ketcham defends himself by saying that all his characters are caricatures. He then wrote,

> Dennis' friend, Jackson, Is black. I drew him black, feeling confident that in cartooning as in life, black is beautiful. He's a caricature, yes, but so are all my cartoon characters. It has not been my intention to offend anyone. Evidently in my effort to improve my design of Jackson, I was mistaken in reading the public heart and mind.[11]

Kecham clearly thought that a Sambo stereotype would not offend, and that his original January 6 figure, not a realistic portrait of an African

American child by any account, was not drawn black. To Ketcham's mind then drawing a figure black required a Sambo figure. This is something Ketcham made explicit in his autobiography saying he "designed him in the tradition of Little Black Sambo with huge lips, big white eyes, and just a suggestion of an afro." In the autobiography Ketcham describes this as his "introductory drawing."[12]

Just how large the protest was about the May 13 comic is unclear. But at best Ketcham again had a bad memory because the St. Louis *Post-Dispatch* did not carry *Dennis the Menace*, not on that day and indeed as far as I can tell never in the 1970s. It is possible that the St. Louis *Globe Democrat*, which had a joint production deal with the *Post*-Dispatch, and was printed at the latter's plant, might have run *Dennis the Menace*. I do not have access to that paper. This may have caused the *Post-Dispatch* to attract protest. But there were no reports of rocks being thrown, or any sort of public protest at its offices, in the *Post-Dispatch* of May 14 or 15, 1970, so it seems unlikely. Ketcham's notion of rocks and bottles being thrown through the windows of the newspaper then was fanciful. Or perhaps he conflated the reaction to his cartoon with the general wave of protest over Nixon's war in Cambodia that swept the country that month and saw four students shot dead at Kent State University, Ohio, by the National Guard on May 4 and two African Americans by the police at Jackson State College in Mississippi on May 15. Certainly, there was some outrage expressed at Ketcham's racist rendition. The *Washington Post* ran the strip in some early edition of the paper on May 13 before pulling it from later editions. *Washington Post* staff writer Chester M. Hampton commented on the comic in the June 6 edition of the paper. After reviewing the sorry history of comic strip and cartoon representations of African Americans he suggested that Hank Ketcham should keep his strip "lily-white" until he could draw an African American "without resorting to racial stereotype."[13] Hampton's piece was picked up by at least two newspapers in Greely, Colorado and Akron, Ohio. Earlier a letter writer to the San Antonio *Express and News* of May 23 had called out Ketcham's comic for its Sambo representation.[14] But the controversy seems not to have generated as much public heat as Ketcham remembers and certainly not the violence. In any case, a search of newspapers at this time for mention of Ketcham turns up more accounts of his third marriage in June 1970 than of this episode.

The British *Dennis* also was mostly free of racial depictions, but they did occur. On November 6, 1954, Dennis attempted to disguise himself with blackface makeup received as part of a disguise outfit from his Auntie Bessie. Law simply rendered Dennis all black, including his normally red striped jersey, and Dad duly failed to recognize him saying, "I'll ask that little black boy if he's seen Dennis!" Dennis makes the mistake of replying, "No Dad!" to his father's question and the strip ends with Dennis getting the slipper. The only reason worth mentioning this strip is that sending a nephew a disguise outfit complete with blackface makeup was, if not the norm, enough of a possibility that Law could use it in his strip. On December 24, 1955, Law had Dennis receive a hot water bottle as a Christmas gift from the same Auntie Bessie. He then proceeds to use the hot water bottle for all sorts of mischief. In the third and fourth panel of the week's strip he encounters "Softy Smith" who is wearing his Christmas gift, a Zulu outfit. Dennis uses the water bottle to spray Smith with a black substance saying, "You can't be a real Zulu warrior without a blackface." And in that panel Law represents Smith as a Sambo type caricature. It is not the heart of the week's gag, but indicative that such humor was available and understood. Indeed, between 1958 and 1978 the BBC broadcast *The Black and White Minstrel Show* complete with blackface performers at least to 1972. In the same period, similarly named stage performances enjoyed widespread popularity.[15] On September 9, 1961, Dennis requests a "Gollywog" [sic] as a gift. The Golliwog first appeared in an 1895 book *The Adventures of Two Dutch Dolls and a Golliwogg* and was yet another instance of blackface minstrelsy. In this episode Dennis uses the Golliwog to take his place in bed to fool his father so that he could slip out and cause mischief, but have an alibi. Again race is not at the core of the strip, except that the Golliwog was such a familiar figure in Britain. Indeed, the resemblance between the Golliwog's hair and Dennis the Menace's as shown in this episode raises the possibility that Dennis's creators might have been subconsciously riffling on the theme and created a whiteface Golliwog. One episode though is not evidence enough to conclude a connection.

Race may seem absent from the two *Dennis the Menace* comics since representations of black figures happens so seldom in the period between 1951 and 1963 and indeed not at all in the American feature. But in some ways, this was all the more telling of the presence of race. The absence of black figures in Dennis's neighborhood is a reminder of the 1950s in America as a continuing era of segregation and real estate covenants that prevented African Americans from moving into white suburbs. Black figures may not have been present, but in the American *Dennis the*

Menace race was ever present. The absence of nonwhite figures in the British Dennis was perhaps more understandable in the early years of the comic, but the years under review here were years of some shift in the population. Between 1953 and 1962 almost half a million immigrants arrived in Britain largely from South Asia and the Caribbean. That is, by 1962, when the population was 53.25 million, just under 1% of the population were recently arrived nonwhites.[16] The point here is not that comics should seek to be representative of multiracial societies, but that Ketcham and Law mostly avoided race-based jokes in their strips. But on the extremely rare occasion that they used them these were stereotypical representations. And in Ketcham's case he made a deliberate choice to shift from a somewhat less offensive caricature to an extremely offensive caricature based on what he thought in meant to draw "black." Both artists had the racial stereotype trope at their disposal, but the circumstance to use it was disappearing.

DIFFERENCES IN FORM

Beyond the difference between a weekly strip in a children's comics magazine and a panel feature in the daily newspaper the two comics had some significant differences in form that separate the sort and style of themes they worked. The British *Dennis the Menace* lived in a fantastical world in which familiar figures such as parents, teachers, and policeman existed and sought to enforce rules. But Dennis himself lived outside of those rules and when he came into contact with the world, order seemed to dissolve, and order was not simply a social and political order, but the rules of the physical world. For instance, in the barber story of May 24, 1952, a boy standing on Dennis's shoulders and wearing a long coat will be mistaken for an adult barber by Dennis's father. Something fantastical happens in almost every episode. So in an episode selected at random from January 14, 1961, Dennis adds a giant spring to a pogo stick (jumping stick in Britain) and can leap high enough to use his peashooter on a pair in a glider. Using the second week of January as a test for the existence of fantastical elements in Dennis January 13, 1962, has a fly literally going down in flames after being sprayed, a minor but still out-of-this-world event. Tracking back to 1952, the January 12 issue had Dad wearing a fish bowl as a helmet to overcome the pepper Dennis has placed on his backside to cause Dad to sneeze while disciplining him with a slipper. On January 9, 1954,

Dennis blows a tire up to gigantic proportions. The next year on January 8 Dennis's constant victim, Walter, by happenstance manages to pull a tablecloth out from a fully laden table disturbing nothing, not exactly fantastical, but unlikely. Nothing fantastical happened in the issue of January 28, 1956 (the first available to me) but Dad does imagine Dennis capable of using a cannon to blow people's heads off. The episodes of 1958 and 1959 likewise contain fantastical elements, but not the 1957 episode. In the episode of January 9, 1960, Dennis goes all out stealing two cannons and a portcullis from a museum, mounting the canons in his house windows and digging a moat around the house. For a time, from mid-1959, Law strove to incorporate some fantastic element from the week in the title of the strip. So on May 30, 1959, the strip's title appears in an outset title panel that consists of Dennis's head encased in a German World War I helmet, the spike of which is the key element in the week's story. On March 25, 1961, Dennis appears in the title panel as a cross between himself, a sunflower, and a Venus flytrap. This sort of fantastical landscape then called for a certain type of story. The British *Dennis* had two essential features: First, as much mayhem as possible in as an inventive a fashion as Law could devise in any given week and second, Dennis's inevitable punishment by slipper. The punishment by slipper is so much a part of the comic that sometimes Law could work his gag, as in the January 28, 1956, cannon story by having Dennis escape such punishment for once.

The American *Dennis the Menace* instead was a gag strip. The structure of a single-panel, six days a week set Dennis up as having a series of situations that a gag could revolve around; for instance, the broken window, the inappropriate comment, the sexual innuendo, the barber, the cookie jar, being sent to face the corner for bad behavior, cowboys, and the babysitter. That Dennis would be a difficult customer for baby-sitters is a given. How that plays out, that is how Ketcham and his staff could find the gag in that situation, is the way the comic operated. Just as Law had to move his Dennis to the slipper in the final panel, Ketcham had to work a series of situations for the humor. In the first two years of the American *Dennis* Ketcham used 13 babysitter jokes. In the first on June 16, 1951, Alice is on the phone. She says, "Billie Jean? Listen, dear, would you come over and sit with... Hello? Hello?" This gag fit the broader theme of Dennis's reputation preceding him, but Ketcham did not stay within those bounds for his babysitter gags. On July 11, Dennis surmises to a playmate that the trouble his folks have in getting a sitter is that they do not pay enough. On September 1, Henry gives a sitter a list of emergency numbers and the location of the first-aid kit. On September 27, this Dennis as a problem for the sitter trope shifts to the babysitter as the problem when Dennis says to his father, "Can I sit up until her boy friend comes over about half-hour after you've gone?" On November 30, the gag shifts back to Dennis as a problem with the sitter calling Alice for advice on how to make Dennis go to bed – a club. And on December 13 as Alice and Henry drive away from home she hopes Dennis will not cause the sitter too many problems especially since he hid before they left. Dennis looks on from the back seat. This gag drew on another standard gag Ketcham used in which Dennis would be standing behind Alice unexpectedly when, for instance, as on October 21, 1953, she was telling a school teacher on the phone to check that Dennis was not hiding behind the teacher. Several other episodes followed in 1952 using the basic theme and then on May 9 Ketcham found another type of babysitter gag: the sheer pleasure of the parents to get away for some time. Babysitter gags were a constant for Ketcham who found ways to work this trope and its variations for years. In early 1962 he hit a purple patch with gags on February 2, March 2, March 30, and April 28. The March 30 strip with Dennis attending a dinner party with his parents because they had run out of sitters was indicative of this group of strips.

The American Dennis also had a Sunday comic strip incarnation. This strip differed from the daily feature not only in having a series of panels, but also in using word balloons. Together, the use of sequential panels and word balloons would have changed the way readers processed the strip. On the one hand the processes involved in looking at a single panel with text below and on the other hand looking at a series of panels that use word balloons would differ. Moving from a single panel also meant that unlike the daily comic that simply delivered a gag, the Sunday strip had to offer a humorous narrative or unfold a gag over several panels. The Sunday strip then was quite distinct from the daily, perhaps more so than the Sunday *Skippy* strips from the dailies and the Perry Winkle Sundays from the daily *Winnie Winkle* strip. The daily comic even at is most complex with panels within the single panel, such as the January 5, 1961, episode where Ketcham used a door-frame and perspective to create the sense of several separate panels, had an uncluttered look. The Sunday strips seemed boxy and closed in with the word balloons occupying space Ketcham normally used to create a sense of depth (Fig. 4.2).

Fig. 4.2   *Dennis the Menace, Washington Post,* March 22, 1959

THE QUESTION OF CLASS

The British *Dennis the Menace* looked more to raucous funny papers antecedents such as *Ally Sloper's Half Holiday* (1884–1916), and indeed forward to the crude broad adult humor of *Viz* (1979-), than did his American counterpart.[17] The American *Dennis*, rather than looking to the equally raucous antecedent Yellow Kid, looked to the toned down and domesticated *Buster Brown*.[18] James Parker, a contributing editor to *The Atlantic*, discussing the two *Dennis* comics wrote, the

American Dennis radiated the irrepressible energy of a young republic. In contrast, British Dennis represented a form of transgression that didn't even exist in the United States. He emerged during a time of class struggle and waning empire, when the U.K. establishment feared the oik, the yob, the ungovernable prole. In short, British Dennis was a proto-punk-rock-hooligan.[19]

Parker's view is far too simplistic and the language he, or his editor, couched the comparison plays to American exceptionalism. So the American *Dennis* is "lovable" and a product of America's "irrepressible energy." The British *Dennis* is "evil," "sinister," and "transgressive" in ways unknown to Americans. The waning British Empire is an easy mark, but the notion of an establishment fearful of governing a working class should be balanced against a return to power of the Conservative Party under Winston Churchill in 1951. Conversely, strike activity did increase in the years between 1951 and 1964, although not uniformly.[20] Moreover, the British *Dennis* seems to be middle class, or at very least white collar working class with middle-class aspirations, since his Dad in these years always wore a suit. Dennis's Dad also owned a car and a caravan (camper trailer) before Dennis destroyed the latter on August 14, 1954. Owning a car in the early 1950s in Britain was not yet a common thing and indicative of a higher income than average. The British Dennis's stock in trade was anarchic mischief. This was meted out fairly even-handedly to anyone he came across. Figures of authority such as school teachers, parents, and policeman may have been the target of many of his pranks, but so too were fellow students, the postman (April 18, 1959), circus performers (10 times between 1952 and 1962), lorry drivers (March 13, 1954), painters (January 22, 1955), paper mill workers (May 18, 1957), train drivers (April 25, 1959), and commuters waiting to take a bus (October 10, 1959). And the list could go on. The point is that seeing Dennis as demonstrative of some sort of class warfare unknown to America is misguided.

The American *Dennis's* family had all the accoutrements of a middle-class family. His father worked in an office with a secretary (November 24, 1952), and they had a suburban home and owned a car. In the early years of the comic Ketcham did offer some jokes about the problems of salary earners. For instance, on November 20, 1951, Henry tells Alice about asking for a raise and suggests to Dennis that he play outside for a while since clearly his boss did not respond well to the request. On April 29, 1953, Dennis holding his piggybank wonders aloud why it is always lighter at the end of the month. His parents steadfastly ignore his question. On February 26, 1953, Henry takes Dennis with him to visit the Credit Loan Corporation. Dennis asks the manager, "You won't really take my Daddy's right arm, will you, Mister?" These sorts of gags became less frequent as the strip aged and the focus of the gag was less to do with the need for income as the results of having it. So by January 4, 1961, Dennis tells Henry who is sitting with his accountant, "'In come Tex' don't sound right to me. Shouldn't you say 'Tex came in'?"

The differences between the two *Dennis the Menaces* then come down to three factors: history, form, and readership. Comics as a medium developed in different ways in Britain and the British *Dennis* appearing in a comic weekly, in strip form, aimed at a young readership demonstrated very little influence from American comics. Beyond the use of word balloons to convey speech there are no other discernible influences from American comics. Although Richard Outcault's the Yellow Kid established the importance of a distinctive character in a serial form for American comics *Ally Sloper* had done the same thing in Britain, and earlier.[21] The American *Dennis*, while centered on a distinctive character, came just as much from a tradition associated with the gag cartoon in general circulation magazines. Indeed, rather than using word balloons the daily feature carried the spoken word as below-the-panel text. The American *Dennis's* status as a comic relies on its featured character, it regular appearance, its place on the comics page, and its Sunday episodes (in a different style) for its status as a comic strip. That two comics, which on the surface share so much, can be so different reminds us that shared genre does not equate to the sameness or commonality of comic strips.

NOTES

1. "Dennis the Menace," *Don Markstein's Toonopedia*, http://www.toonope dia.com/dennisb.htm.
2. Jonathan Petrie, "Scrawled on a Pack of Players, Dennis the Very First Menace," *Daily Mail*, September 6, 2009, http://www.dailymail.co.uk/news/article-1211390/Scrawled-pack-Players-Dennis-Menace.html.
3. Brian Walker, "Introduction," *Hank Ketcham's Complete Dennis the Menace 1951–1963* (Seattle: Fantagraphics, 2005), xiv.
4. Lizabeth Cohen, *A Consumer's Republic: The Politics of Mass Consumption in Postwar America* (New York: Knopf, 2003); Gavin Mackenzie, "The Economic Dimensions of Embourgeoisement," *British Journal of Sociology*, Vol. 18 (1967): 29–44.
5. Ina Zweiniger-Bargielowska, "Rationing, Austerity and the Conservative Party Recovery After 1945," *Historical Journal*, Vol. 37, No. 1 (1994): 173–197.

6. Ian Gordon, *Comic Strips and Consumer Culture* (Washington, DC: Smithsonian Institution Press, 1998), 89.

7. *The Beano*, https://www.dcthomson.co.uk/brands/the-beano/.

8. Stephen Armstrong, "Was Pixar's Inside Out inspired by The Beano?," *Telegraph*, July 27, 2015, http://www.telegraph.co.uk/culture/pixar/11766202/Was-Pixars-Inside-Out-inspired-by-The-Beano.html.

9. Gerard Jones, *Men of Tomorrow: Geeks, Gangsters, and the Birth of the Comic Book* (New York: Basic Books, 2005), 94 and 105.

10. Hank Ketcham, *The Merchant of Dennis* (New York: Abbeville Press, 1990), 191–192.

11. Hank Ketcham, "Letter to the Editor," *Indianapolis Star*, May 22, 1970, 27. Also in *Tucson Daily Citizen*, June 9, 1970, 23.

12. Ketcham, *The Merchant of Dennis*, 191

13. Chester M. Hampton, "Times Change But Old Stereotypes Die Hard," *Washington Post*, June 6, 1970, A14.

14. Chester M. Hampton, "Racial Stereotype Surfaces Again in Newspaper Cartoon," *Greeley Daily Tribune*, June 10, 1970, 4; Chester M. Hampton, "Blacks in Cartoons Deserve Reality," *Akron Beacon Journal*, June 14, 1970, 99. Harold E. Baliste Jr., "'Black Sambo' Caricature," *Express and News* (San Antonio, TX), May 23, 1970, 26.

15. "Obituary: Robert Luff," *The Telegraph*, February 23, 2009, http://www.telegraph.co.uk/news/obituaries/4788794/Robert-Luff.html.

16. Zig Latyton-Henry, "The New Commonwealth Migrants: 1945–62," *History Today*, Vol. 35, No. 12 (December 1985): 27–33.

17. Roger Sabin, "Ally Sloper: The First Comics Superstar?," *Image and Narrative*, Vol. 4, No. 1 (October 2003), http://www.imageandnarrative.be/inarchive/graphicnovel/rogersabin.htm; Nicholas Lezard, "The Modern Hogarths," *The Guardian*, December 18, 2004, https://www.theguardian.com/books/2004/dec/18/comics.

18. Gordon, *Comic Strips and Consumer Culture*, 37–58.

19. James Parker, "Dennis the Menace Has an Evil British Twin: Meet the Lovable American Cartoon Character's Sinister Counterpart," *Smithsonian Magazine*, March 2016, http://www.smithsonianmag.com/arts-culture/dennis-menace-has-evil-british-twin-180958114/#oHP56A0pRB4bbb4Z.99.

20. P. Galambos and E. W. Evans, "Work-Stoppages in The United Kingdom, 1951–1964: A Quantitative Study," *Bulletin of the Oxford University Institute of Economics & Statistics*, Vol. 28, No. 1 (1966): 33–57.

21. David Kunzle, "Marie Duval: A Caricaturist Rediscovered," *Woman's Art Journal*, Vol. 7, No. 1 (Spring–Summer, 1986): 26–31; Sabin, "Ally Sloper."

CHAPTER 5

Comics Scholarship and Comparative Studies

Abstract This chapter offers a brief overview of other ways to approach comparative studies of comics.

Keywords Translation · Manga · Political economy · Formal qualities

This book compares kid comics in different countries to discuss the international histories of the medium. Even as such a study reveals differences in cultures it shows some commonalities of the form and jokes. In comics like the two *Dennis the Menaces* that are disparate in so many ways, despite the similarities of name and theme, it is still odd the way that something as obvious as a babysitter joke never appears in the British version. Since I could not find all the issues of *The Beano* for the period under examination I cannot be sure a babysitter joke never appeared, but they certainly did not appear at the frequency of the American counterpart. This seeming oddity might help explain cultural differences. From reading the two *Dennis* comics the lack of babysitter jokes in the British version suggests that one or some of these things distinguished British from American society in the 1950s and early 1960s: the British were more inclined to leave older children at home by themselves, there is no tradition of babysitter jokes in Britain, middle-class Britons in the period preferred to stay at home in the evening, dinner parties were not a British thing, dining out for the British middle class was not as frequent as for the American middle class, and/or the impact of rationing

© The Author(s) 2016
I. Gordon, *Kid Comic Strips*, Palgrave Studies in Comics and Graphic Novels, DOI 10.1057/978-1-137-55580-9_5

during World War II was still so deeply felt that behavior of not inviting people into the home had become socially ingrained because of an inability to share what had been a limited availability of foodstuffs. The point here is that a comparative study of the comic reveals what artists and writers thought would work in the culture in question. This tells us about the relationship between comics' content and the society around it, and by extension a comparison tells us the way different senses of comic humor derived from and influenced the culture. Comparative studies of comics genres, which beyond kid comics include among others, adventure, Western, romance, gag, science fiction, funny animals, and detective strips, offers a productive method for understanding how different forms of narrative work in comics in different countries. As far as the kid comics under consideration in this book are concerned, since all of them are humorous in nature, the comparison shows us what people found funny in the four countries in question, or at least in as far as a comic could generate humor.

Genre is but one way of approaching comparative studies of comics. Another way, touched on in this work, is studies of comics' translations. Several scholars have followed this path with much of the work in the field of translation studies, rather than comic studies per se. Cultural anthropologist, Drew Hopkins's fascinating study of *Dilbert's* Taiwanese incarnation accounts for cultural difference in the form of work and management, and the careful selection of Chinese characters to represent the various cast members of that strip. Hopkins pays attention to the Chinese tonal structure of Dilbert's Chinese name *Daibote* for the various meanings it conveys. To make the comic work in Taiwan, translators positioned it, much more than in America, as a critique of jargon and the blind belief of Taiwanese entrepreneurs in jargon's power.[1] Heike Elisabeth Jüngst deals with issues involved in translating manga to German. Unlike most Western comics, manga are read right to left both in the meta form of the book and the immediate form of panels on a page. Jüngst found that translating decisions came to depend more on fan expectations than on translators' judgments to the extent that German comics produced "feigned authenticity" by being produced to be read right to left so preserving some sense of their Japaneseness.[2] Adele D'Arcangelo and Federico Zanettin analyze the translation of the Italian comic *Dylan Dog* for the American market and discuss the impact that changing visual elements has on verbal elements.[3] Coming at comparative studies of comics through issues of translation offers some particularly useful insights because the issues are larger than what does and does not translate from one country to another. Such studies have to deal with the interplay between the visual and the text and how to shift one is to shift the other. Translations to and from Chinese also have the additional problem, or opportunity, of the sort of word play that might be created through associations through the tonal coding of Chinese.

Another way of doing comparative work on comics and their international dimensions is to look at the political economy of their production as they move from one culture to another. Casey Brienza has produced a host of work in this field with her *Manga in America: Transnational Book Publishing and the Domestication of Japanese Comics*, a magisterial work based on detailed interviews with American industry figures she delineates that way in which the processes of making manga available to American audiences shifts their content, domesticating manga in America and making all manga more American. Brienza has also edited a volume of the spread of manga to other nations and the essays in this volume too engage with its domestication elsewhere.[4] In a related project, scholars and Jacqueline Berndt have conducted several academic conferences across Asia on the spread of women's manga beyond Japan. Associated with this project, Lim Cheng Tju has sketched a comparative outline of comics by women in Southeast Asia.[5] Kevin Patrick takes a somewhat similar approach of tracing the domestication of The Phantom in his forthcoming 2017 University of Iowa Press book *The Phantom Unmasked: America's First Superhero and Global Comics Culture*, which traces the characters distinctive incarnations in Australia, India, and Sweden.

An international comparison of comics could also examine different use of formal aspects of comics such as word balloons. As mentioned in Chapter 1, both Thierry Smolderen and Pascal Lefèvre have already conducted such studies. Smolderen traces the development of these instruments from the viewpoint of their function and shape and size. Lefèvre traces their introduction in comics in different countries.[6] A detailed study of the Italian versions of Buster Brown (*Mimmo Mammolo*) in *Corriere dei Piccoli* that focused on the removal of word balloons and the use of rhyming captions in their place would tell us much about the different forms of the humor to be had from Buster's antics and attitudes toward childhood.

This book in comparing American comic strips to strips in Australia, France, and Britain is partially a provocation to those who still insist on the unique Americanness of comic strips as an art form. It is also an argument for understanding the American contribution to the development of comics as largely the commercialization of the form in ways that could be readily adapted to the comics' traditions of other countries. And it is a reminder that so much humor both good (balls through window gags) and bad (racist stereotypes) is international in character even as it plays out slightly differently in various cultures.

NOTES

1. Drew Hopkins, "The Dilberting of Taiwan," *Connect*, Vol. 1 (Fall 2000): 151–160.
2. Heike Elisabeth Jüngst, "Japanese Comics in Germany," *Perspectives: Studies in Translatology*, Vol. 12, No. 2 (2004): 83–105.
3. Adele D'Arcangelo and Federico Zanettin, "Dylan Dog Goes to The USA: A North American Translation of an Italian Comic Book Series," *Across Languages And Cultures*, Vol. 5, No. 2 (2004): 187–210. See also, Federico Zanettin, "Comics in Translation Studies: An Overview and Suggestions for Research," in Vlle Seminaire de Traduction Scientifique et Technique en Langue Portugaise, *Tradução e interculturalismo: actas do seminário* (Lisbon: União Latina, 2005): 93–98.
4. Casey Brienza, *Manga in America: Transnational Book Publishing and the Domestication of Japanese Comics* (London: Bloomsbury Academic, 2016) and *Global Manga: Japanese Comics Without Japan?* (Burlington, VT: Ashgate, 2015).
5. Fusami Ogi, Lim Cheng Tju, and Jacqueline Berndt, eds, "Women's Manga Beyond Japan: Contemporary Comics as Cultural Crossroads in Asia," *International Journal of Comic Art*, Vol. 13, No. 2 (2011): 1–199 and Lim Cheng Tju, "Stories by Female Comic Artists in Southeast Asia," in *International Perspectives on Shojo and Shojo Manga: The Influence of Girl Culture*, Masami Toku, editor (New York: Routledge, 2015), 77–86.
6. Thierry Smolderen, "Of Labels, Loops, and Bubbles: Solving the Historical Puzzle of the Speech Balloon," *Comic Art*, No. 8 (Summer 2006): 90–113; Pascal Lefèvre, The Battle Over the Balloon: The Conflictual Institutionalization of the Speech Balloon in Various European Cultures," *Image & Narrative*, Vol. 14 (July 2006), http://www.imageandnarrative.be/inarchive/painting/pascal_levevre.htm.

INDEX

© The Author(s) 2016   91
I. Gordon, *Kid Comic Strips*, Palgrave Studies in Comics
and Graphic Novels, DOI 10.1057/978-1-137-55580-9

Printed by Printforce, the Netherlands